The JIST Job Search Course

A Young Person's Guide to Getting & Keeping a

Learn to:

- Prepare for future career and job changes
- Meet an employer's expectations
- Identify your skills
- Look at and organize your past experiences
- Complete superior applications and resumes
- Locate the best jobs for you
- Use effective job search techniques
- Organize your time to get a good job in less time
- Get ahead on a new job

IMPORTANT NOTE TO TEACHERS AND INSTRUCTORS

This book was written to support a course on career planning, job search methods and job survival skills for high school juniors and seniors. The course can be presented as a "mini" curriculum within a variety of other courses (such as Social Studies or English) or as a separate course.

A separate instructor's guide is available to support this book and is essential for its presentation in a class or group setting. It will save you many hours of session planning and preparation. Teachers and instructors should contact the publisher for a copy of this comprehensive guide if it is not already available. It contains specific in-class activities to support each chapter of this book as well as suggested homework, transparency and handout masters, discussion topics, and more.

JIST also has a catalog of over 500 career related materials including books, videos, assessment tests, software and instructional aids. They are all carefully reviewed and selected from over 40 sources and are among the best in the field. Contact us for a free copy of our current catalog, to obtain information on staff training, or request to be added to our mailing list. Or just to chat.

Project Director/Interior Design: Spring Dawn Reader
Editor: Greg Croy
Production Editor: Lisa Farr
Calligraphy: Debb Hibbs
Cover Design: Al Smith
Art Panels Writer/Illustrator: David R. Lister
Spot Illustrations: Mike Kreffel
Manuscript Preparation: Mary Croy

The JIST Job Search Course: *A Young Person's Guide To Getting and Keeping a Good Job*

Send all inquiries to:

JIST Works, Inc.
720 North Park Avenue • Indianapolis, IN 46202-3431
Phone: **(317) 264-3720** • Fax: **(317) 264-3709**

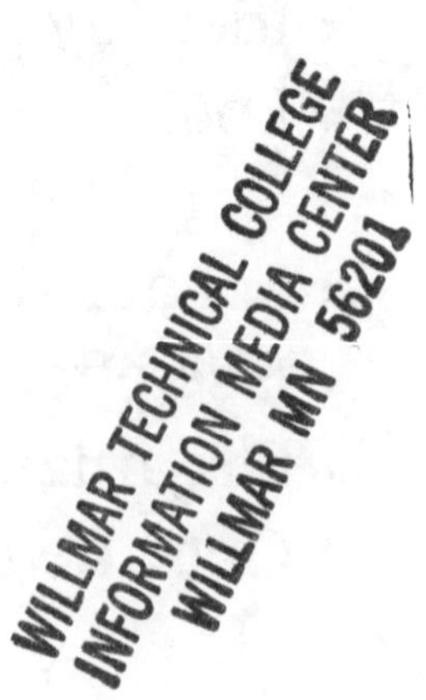

ISBN: 0-942784-34-0

FOREWORD

You are fortunate to attend a program that teaches you the material in this book. Most people are not so fortunate. Neither author, for example, was taught anything about career exploration or job seeking in high school or college. Neither of us took a "career" test or learned about job seeking. In short, no one helped us make career-related decisions. We turned out well, but it could have been so much easier for us if we had been offered this type of training.

While this book is easy to use, you should know that the content is based on extensive research into the most effective career planning, job search methods and job survival skills available. Over 300,000 people have used the same JIST job search techniques to find better jobs in less time. The techniques we recommend DO work! But they will work only if you are willing to use them.

If you plan to get a full-time, summer, or part time job in the next few years, this book will help. We wrote it to give you the basics you need in order to obtain a new job and to do it well. But even if you don't plan to look for a job soon, the material is important for other reasons. It will encourage you to think about what you want out of life and what you have to offer to others. Can you, for example, list your skills and tell someone what you do well? Do you know how to select a job or an educational goal based on what you would like to do? Do you know where to find out about various jobs that interest you? Or which job search methods are the most effective?

You will learn to answer these questions — and many more — in this book. We wish you well.

Mike Farr
Marie Pavlicko

P.S.: The word "JIST" stands for *Job Information & Seeking Training*. It is also the name of an organization of people, JIST Works, Inc., which develops results-oriented job search approaches, trains trainers and publishes career and job search materials — including this book.

ABOUT THE AUTHORS

J. Michael Farr is the president of JIST Works, Inc. His job search books have sold over 300,000 copies and thousands of people have benefited from his results-oriented job search techniques.

Marie Pavlicko coordinates career education for a large school system and has had first-hand experience in teaching JIST techniques to thousands of high school aged students.

The two of them have joined together in developing this comprehensive job search course. Others, including many instructors and students, have contributed their ideas and suggestions for improvements over several revisions. The materials have, literally, been years in the making.

Table of Contents

CHAPTER 1
AN INTRODUCTION TO THE WORLD OF WORK 1
The Stakes Are High 1
The Job Search Quiz 2

CHAPTER 2
AN EMPLOYER'S EXPECTATIONS 5
Anticipating The Employer 5
Employer's Expectation 1—Personal Appearance 7
Employer's Expectation 2—Attendance, Punctuality, Reliability, Dependability 8
Employer's Expectation 3—Skills, Abilities, Interests 8

CHAPTER 3
IDENTIFYING YOUR SKILLS 13
Three Types Of Skills 13
Self-Management Skills 13
Transferable Skills 14
Job-Related Skills 14

CHAPTER 4
THE DATA SEARCH AND *DATA MINDER* 23
Organizing Your "Work" Assets 23
Work References 30
Personal And Professional References 31

CHAPTER 5
AVOID THE APPLICATION TRAP 35
Tips—Completing The Application 35

CHAPTER 6
JIST CARDS: A MINI-RESUME 45
The Mini-Resume 45
What Do You Think? 46
Some Ways You Can Use A *JIST Card* 46
The Anatomy Of A *JIST Card* 47
Tips—Creating Your Own *JIST Card* 47
Sample *JIST Cards* 48

CHAPTER 7

FINDING JOB LEADS 53

Job Leads—The Hows, Whats, Whens, And Wheres **53**
Where To Find Job Leads 54
Informal Job Search Methods 54
Cold Contacts: Contacting Employers Directly 58
Traditional Job Search Methods 60
The Answers For How People Find Jobs 61

CHAPTER 8

DIALING FOR DOLLARS: USING THE TELEPHONE 65

Why The Telephone? **65**
You Can Do It! 65
A Sample Telephone Script 66
The 6 Parts to a JIST Phone Script 66
Telephone Contact Goals 68
Learning To Overcome Typical Problems 68

CHAPTER 9

THE INTERVIEW 73

The Interview And Employer's Expectations **73**
Appearance 73
Dependability 74
Skills 74
A Technique For Answering Interview Questions 74
A Sample Response 74
Questions You Might Ask An Employer 78
Closing The Interview 78
After The Interview: Follow Up! 79

CHAPTER 10

SUPERIOR RESUMES, COVER LETTERS, AND THANK-YOU NOTES 81

Types Of Resumes **81**
The Chronological Resume 81
Sample Chronological Resumes: Judith Jones 82
The Skills And Combination Resumes 86
The Cover Letter 90
Thank-You Notes and Letters 91

CHAPTER 11

ORGANIZING YOUR JOB SEARCH 95

The Objective Of Your Job Search: To Get Interviews 95
Part One: Basic Decisions 96
Part Two: Creating Your Weekly And Daily Job Search Calendar 98
Weekly Job Search Schedule Worksheet 100
The JIST Job Search Course Review 102
A Formula For Job Search Success 104

CHAPTER 12

SURVIVING ON A NEW JOB AND GETTING AHEAD 107

Success On The Job 107
Appearance 107
Dependability 108
Skills 109
Other Expectations 110
Why People Get Fired 111
The Reasons People Are Fired: The Employer's Point Of View 112
It's Not Always Your Fault 113
Advanced Tips—Moving Up The Career Ladder 113
Leaving A Job 115
Sample Resignation Letter 116

ADDENDUM: GETTING CAREER INFORMATION—FIGURING OUT A JOB OBJECTIVE 118

Exploring Careers 118
Counseling Resources 118
Printed Resources 119
Human Resources 120
Occupational Outlook Handbook Occupations Listing 120

CHAPTER 1

AN INTRODUCTION TO THE WORLD OF WORK

You probably already know some things about finding a job. Perhaps you have found part-time jobs in the past. Before looking for a job, you should also have some idea of what type of job you are qualified for.

Your job now is to learn how to find a good job and how to find it in less time. In order to be successful in this venture, you must know how to identify your present skills, learn some new ones, and improve the job search techniques you already know.

The Stakes Are High

During the years that you work, you will probably change jobs and even careers many times. Knowing how to find a good job is a valuable skill that can make a difference in your career and your life. Many job seekers have never learned effective job-seeking skills. In fact, over 90 percent have never even read a book on how to find a job. As a result, they often are unemployed far longer than they need to be. And they often take jobs that don't give them the pay and satisfaction another job might.

This course will show you how to organize your job search in a systematic way. Thousands of people have used these job search methods to find better jobs in less time. And so can you.

Like other things you have learned, this course will require some effort. But the advantages to you are great. Whether you are presently working, looking for work, planning to enter the job market upon graduation, or planning to further your education beyond high school, you need to know the basics of how to find a job.

Getting a job *is* a job in itself. The harder you work at it, the better your chances of getting the job you want.

The Job Search Quiz

This job search quiz is designed to find out what you already know about looking for work. It is a learning experience, and there will be no grade given on your answers. Read each question carefully, and answer it as well as you can.

1. What do you think are the top five reasons that people stay unemployed?

____

____

____

____

____

2. What are the top three reasons that employers give for screening out (disqualifying) job seekers?

____

____

____

3. How many weeks is the average job seeker unemployed?

____

4. List five of your best or most important skills. (*Note:* These skills don't have to be job related. They should be things you do particularly well.)

____

____

____

____

____

5. What are the two most effective techniques for finding a job?

____

____

6. How many hours per week should you invest in a job search?

____

7. Guess how often the average person changes jobs.

____

8. How often will the average worker change careers in his or her lifetime?

____

9. What percentage of all jobs is advertised?

____

10. What is the real purpose of an application form?

____

____

11. What size organizations hire the most people?

____

12. What is the present employment rate in your region?

____

GREAT EXPECTATIONS

or

"WHAT THE DICKENS DO EMPLOYERS WANT?"

CONTINUED ON PAGE 11

CHAPTER 2

AN EMPLOYER'S EXPECTATIONS

Sometimes, the best way to know what employers expect of us is to find out what they are looking for in others.

This chapter will help you find out what employers are looking for in job seekers. By taking on the role of the employer, you are going to examine just what employers are looking for in the people they hire.

Anticipating The Employer

ACTIVITY What Does An Employer Expect?

In this activity, you will work with a small group of other students to form your own "company." You are to complete the following tasks:

1. Give your group a company name and product or service.
2. Appoint a group member to be a company "recorder." Make a list of things you think are important to look for in a potential employee. Make your list as long as possible. (Try to list 15 to 20 things.) Your list can also include things that would prevent a person from being hired by your company.
3. Have the recorder list all the ideas your group comes up with.

Use the following worksheet for this activity.

Employee/Employment Characteristics Worksheet

Company Name: ______________________________

Product or Service: ______________________________

____

Types of positions your company is looking to fill: ______________________________

____

List the most important things to look for in a potential employee for the above positions. Don't worry if the ideas seem good or bad; just list every idea that anyone in your group has.

______________________ ______________________

______________________ ______________________

______________________ ______________________

______________________ ______________________

______________________ ______________________

______________________ ______________________

______________________ ______________________

______________________ ______________________

______________________ ______________________

______________________ ______________________

______________________ ______________________

______________________ ______________________

In Conclusion

List the key points from other groups that were not in your group's top three ideas.

____

____

____

____

____

____

____

ACTIVITY The Three Major Employer Expectations

Employers know what they expect from people who are applying for jobs. The important question you need to answer is, "Do you meet their expectations?"

Before you answer this, take a closer look at yourself. Are there things that you can improve? Let's review the major things an employer looks for in an interview. Make notes on each one to help you prepare for job interviews.

Employer's Expectation 1—*Personal Appearance*

1. **Do you look like the right person for the job?**
   - How would you dress for an interview?
   - Who in the room looks like the best person for the job, based on the way he or she looks right now (sits, stands, talks, etc.)?
   - What special qualities about that person stand out and make him or her look as if he or she fits the part?
   - What would you do to make a good "first impression"?
2. **Would your manner make the interviewer want to hire you?**
   - How does the way you normally act compare with the way you would act during an interview?
   - What can you do to avoid becoming nervous in an interview?
   - Is it better to be quiet and "shy" in an interview or more assertive—and possibly be seen as "pushy" by an employer?
   - What interview behaviors might an employer react to in a negative way?
3. **How else can you make an impression? How could each of the following impress an employer?**
   - Your paper tools (applications, resumes, etc.).
   - Phone conversations with the employer.
   - What others say about you.

In Conclusion

First impressions count! Did you know that of all job seekers, 40 percent get rejected because of poor personal appearance? If you do not make a positive first impression with an employer, you probably won't get hired.

Assignment

Write three things that you could improve on to meet Employer's Expectation 1.

1. ______________________________
2. ______________________________
3. ______________________________

Employer's Expectation 2—*Attendance, Punctuality, Reliability, Dependability*

1. Can you be counted on to do the job?

- Have you been reliable in the past, either in school or on a previous job? Give examples.
- Why would an employer be interested in your attendance record?
- Why is an employer interested in how long you might stay on the job?
- When is the best time to arrive for an interview? Why?
- What does the expression "Time is money" mean to you?

In Conclusion

Employers will not hire someone unless they are sure they can depend on the person to get the job done. Someone who is unreliable or who will leave too soon after learning the job is not worth the trouble of hiring and training. Many employers will hire a person with fewer "credentials" over a more experienced person if they feel that the inexperienced person is more reliable.

Assignment

Give examples of how you would show an employer that you:

Have a good attendance record.

____

____

Are punctual and reliable.

____

____

Employer's Expectation 3—*Skills, Abilities, Interests*

If you make a good first impression and convince the employer that you can be counted on (Expectations 1 and 2), then your ability to do the job becomes important. Here are some things to consider:

1. What can you do now that relates to a job you want?

   ____

2. Why is the following statement not a good answer to the preceding question? "I worked as a cashier at Ford two years, and I worked as a grill cook at Wendy's two years."

   ____

3. Will employers accept training, hobbies, and other unpaid experiences to make up for a lack of paid work experience? Why?

   ____

4. How could you use job-related training in place of work experience to convince employers to hire you?

____

5. What should you do if your hobbies do not have any relationship at all to the job you want? What if they do?

____

6. Why is it important to translate "life experiences" into informal training and state them in years (or months)?

____

7. What would volunteer work tell an employer about you?

____

In Conclusion

Job-related skills are important to an employer. Most employers will consider training and other life experience to make up for shortcomings in work experience. Many employers will hire a person who they are convinced will be reliable and hard working. They can train this kind of person on the job to make up for any shortcomings.

Assignment

Write three things you could say to an employer in an interview to help meet Employer's Expectation 3.

1. ____________________________________
2. ____________________________________
3. ____________________________________

ACTIVITY Survey Of Employers

This activity will give you an opportunity to learn what local employers look for. You are to visit or call at least one employer before the next class. The employer can be someone you already know—like an uncle, for example. You can also look up an employer in the *Yellow Pages* of the phone book or simply drop in on one on your way home.

As you make your call or visit, use the following survey form to record your information. You will report your findings at the next class session.

Tips—Important Reminders

- Get to the person in charge.
- List the name of the person in charge.
- Ask the three survey questions.
- Record responses on the survey sheet.
- Be ready to report your findings to the class at the next session.

Employer's Expectations Telephone/On-Site Survey Worksheet

Organization Name: ______________________________

Address: ______________________________

Phone: ______________________________

Contact Person: ______________________________

Contact Person's Title: ______________________________

What You Should Do:

Introduce yourself. *Hello, my name is:* ______________________________

I am a student at: ______________________________

Ask to talk to the person in charge, and find out his or her name. *May I please talk to the person in charge*, or *may I speak with Mr. (or Mrs. or Ms.)?* ______________________________

When you speak to that person, introduce yourself again. Explain that you are doing an assignment for school and would like to ask a few questions about what he (or she) looks for in a good worker.

Ask the following three questions, and record the answers in the spaces given.

Could you please tell me what you look for in a person you hire? ______________________________

____

____

____

What are the top three skills needed by the people who work there? ______________________________

____

____

____

What are the most important personality traits for people who do this type of work?

____

____

____

Thank him (or her) for all the help and time spent with you.

CONTINUED FROM PAGE 4

SHERLOCK HOLMES *in an excerpt from...*

THE HOUND OF THE MASTER SKILLS

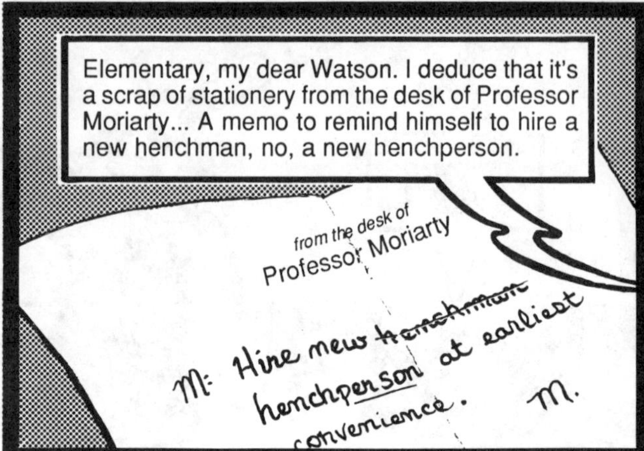

CHAPTER 3

IDENTIFYING YOUR SKILLS

You probably don't realize how many skills you have. In fact, you probably have more than you think.

Employers want to know what skills you will bring to the job. You must be able to identify and give examples of your skills.

Of all job seekers, 80 to 85 percent cannot describe their job skills in an interview. Knowing what you can do well is an important part of your job search and your life.

Three Types Of Skills

How many skills do you have? Write your answer here: ____________.

Each person has hundreds of skills! To better understand them, let's divide them into these three categories:

1. Self-Management Skills
2. Transferable Skills
3. Job-Related Skills

The following are brief definitions of each type of skill.

Self-Management Skills

Self-management skills help you adapt and do well in new situations. They include your personality, your ability to get along with others, and your ability to fit into the work situation. Some examples of using these skills include being reliable, cooperating with others, and being willing to work hard.

Transferable Skills

Transferable skills are those you can use in many different jobs. An auto mechanic, for example, needs to be good with his or her hands, and a secretary must be well organized. These skills can also be used in (or transferred to) many other types of jobs. For example, a carpenter must be good with his or her hands, and a librarian must be well organized.

Job-Related Skills

Job-related skills are needed in a particular job. A secretary, for example, needs to type, and an auto mechanic must be familiar with a variety of tools and repair procedures.

The activities that follow will help you identify your self-management, transferable, and job-related skills. In these sections, be as honest and accurate about yourself as possible. Make sure that you can back up each of your skills with an example!

ACTIVITY Identifying Self-Management Skills

Good Worker Traits

List three things about yourself that, in your opinion, make you a good worker.

1. ______________________________
____

2. ______________________________
____

3. ______________________________
____

Self-Management Skills Checklist

Check all the skills that follow which apply to you.

Key Skills

These are skills all employers value highly. They often won't hire a person who does not have or use most or all of these.

Employers value people who

Skill	Most of the Time	Some of the Time
get to work every day		
arrive on time		
get things done		
follow instructions from supervisor		

Skill	Most of the Time	Some of the Time
get along well with co-workers		
are honest		
work hard		

Self-Management Skills Checklist—continued

Other Self-Management Skills

Skill	Most of the Time	Some of the Time
ambition		
patience		
assertiveness		
learns quickly		
flexibility		
maturity		
dependability		
completes assignments		
sincerity		
solves problems		
friendliness		
a good sense of humor		
physical strength		

Skill	Most of the Time	Some of the Time
highly motivated		
intelligence		
creativity		
leadership		
enthusiasm		
persistence		
self-motivated		
results oriented		
pride in doing a good job		
willingness to learn new things		
takes responsibility		
asks questions		

Other Skills

Add any self-management skills you have that are not on the list.

Additional self-management skills

Skill	Most of the Time	Some of the Time

Skill	Most of the Time	Some of the Time

Your Top Five Self-Management Skills

Now go back through the lists of good worker traits and skills. Circle the five you feel are the most important ones for an employer to know about you.

For each of these five skills, give a good example of when you used that skill. It can be from work, school, family, or another type of experience.

1. Skill:____________ Example: ____________________________________

____

____

2. Skill:____________ Example: ____________________________________

____

____

3. Skill: ____________ Example: ____________________________________

____

____

4. Skill:____________ Example: ____________________________________

____

____

5. Skill:____________ Example: ____________________________________

____

____

For each of these skills, give one example of how you could improve upon it.

1. ____

____

2. ____

____

3. ____

____

4. ____

____

5. ____

____

ACTIVITY Identifying Transferable Skills

Just as in the previous activity, check all the skills that apply to you.

Transferable Skills Checklist

Key Skills

These skills tend to get you higher levels of responsibility and pay. They are worth emphasizing in an interview!

Skill	Most of the Time	Some of the Time
meet deadlines		
speak in public		
supervise others		
accept responsibility		
solve problems		
plan		
understand and control budgets		

Skill	Most of the Time	Some of the Time
increase sales or efficiency		
instruct others		
manage money, budgets		
manage people		
meet deadlines		
meet the public		
organize/manage projects		

Other Transferable Skills

Using my hands/dealing with things

Skill	Most of the Time	Some of the Time
assemble		
build		
construct/repair buildings		
drive/operate vehicles		
good with hands		

Skill	Most of the Time	Some of the Time
observe/inspect		
operate tools, machines		
repair		
use complex equipment		
make things		

Dealing with data

Skill	Most of the Time	Some of the Time
analyze data		
audit records		
budget		
calculate/compute		
check for accuracy		
classify data		

Skill	Most of the Time	Some of the Time
compare		
compile		
count		
detail-oriented		
evaluate		
investigate		

Transferable Skills Checklist—continued

Dealing with data—continued

Skill	Most of the Time	Some of the Time
keep financial records		
locate answers, information		
manage money		
observe/inspect		
record facts		

Skill	Most of the Time	Some of the Time
negotiate		
research		
synthesize		
take inventory		

Working with people

Skill	Most of the Time	Some of the Time
administer		
care for		
confront others		
counsel people		
demonstrate		
diplomatic		
help others		
insight		
instruct		
interview people		
kind		
listen		
negotiate		

Skill	Most of the Time	Some of the Time
outgoing		
patient		
persuade		
pleasant		
sensitive		
sociable		
supervise		
tactful		
teach		
tolerant		
tough		
trust		
understand		

Using words, ideas

Skill	Most of the Time	Some of the Time
articulate		
communicate verbally		
correspond with others		
create new ideas		
design		

Skill	Most of the Time	Some of the Time
edit		
ingenious		
inventive		
library research		
logical		

Transferable Skills Checklist—continued

Using words, ideas—continued

Skill	Most of the Time	Some of the Time
public speaking		
remember information		

Skill	Most of the Time	Some of the Time
write clearly		

Leadership

Skill	Most of the Time	Some of the Time
arrange social functions		
competitive		
decisive		
delegate		
direct others		
explain things to others		
mediate problems		
motivate people		

Skill	Most of the Time	Some of the Time
negotiate agreements		
plan		
results oriented		
risk taker		
run meetings		
self-confident		
self-motivated		
solve problems		

Creative/artistic

Skill	Most of the Time	Some of the Time
artistic		
drawing, art		
expressive		

Skill	Most of the Time	Some of the Time
perform, act		
present artistic ideas		
dance, body movement		

Other Skills

Add any transferable skills that you have that are not on the list.

Additional transferable skills

Skill	Most of the Time	Some of the Time

Skill	Most of the Time	Some of the Time

Your Top Five Transferable Skills

Now go back through the list of skills. Circle the top five that you want to use in the next job you want.

For each of these five skills, give a good example of when you used that skill.

1. Skill:______________Example: ______________________________

2. Skill:______________Example: ______________________________

3. Skill:______________Example: ______________________________

4. Skill:______________Example: ______________________________

5. Skill:______________Example: ______________________________

For each of these skills, give one example of how you could improve on it.

1. ____

2. ____

3. ____

4. ____

5. ____

ACTIVITY Identifying Job-Related Skills

Each job requires skills related to that particular job. A computer programmer needs to understand various computer languages. A cashier needs to know how to make change and use a cash register. Some job-related skills can be learned quickly, while others may take years of training. These skills are *in addition to* the transferable and self-management skills needed to succeed in that job.

Even if you have not yet actually worked in the job you want, you probably have some "experience" that relates to it. This usually comes from several sources:

- Courses you have taken
- Other jobs or volunteer work
- Hobbies, family activities, and other experiences

You should have some idea of the type of job you want. Use the space below to write the job title of that job.

____

In the spaces below, list some job-related skills you have that relate to this job.

1. Job-related skills I have gained from my school courses or vocational training:

____

____

____

2. Job-related skills I have used in other work or volunteer experiences:

____

____

____

3. Job-related skills I have gained in hobbies, family activities, or other experiences outside of work or school:

____

____

____

These sources of job-related skills are covered in more detail in Chapter 4.

THE HOUND OF THE MASTER SKILLS

2

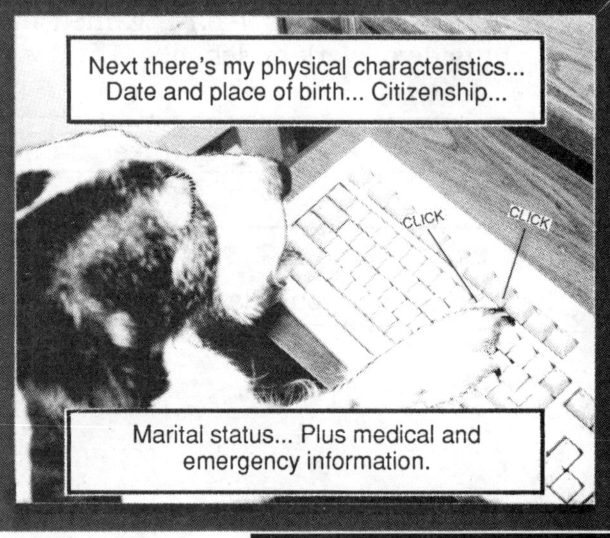

CONTINUED ON PAGE 33

CHAPTER 4

THE DATA SEARCH AND *DATA MINDER*

*Telling an employer you can do a job is not enough. You have to **prove** you can do the job by showing the potential employer concrete examples of your experience and knowledge. These examples can come from many different areas including work, paid and unpaid, school, hobbies, and everyday life.*

In each of the activities that follow, think about the things an employer might want to know about you. Responsibilities and skills are examples of employer concerns.

Organizing Your "Work" Assets

ACTIVITY Evaluating Your Work Experience

This activity collects information on jobs you have had. Include any part-time or summer job here, even if you worked for only a short time. If you don't have much paid work experience, use the same form for unpaid volunteer or informal work, such as helping in the family business, mowing lawns, baby-sitting or similar activities.

Start with the most recent job and work backward. Include all your jobs even if they were for a brief period of time. Use additional sheets as necessary.

Job:______________________________ From:__________ To:__________

Job:______________________________ From:__________ To:__________

Job:______________________________ From:__________ To:__________

Select two of these jobs and complete a Volunteer/Paid Work Experience Worksheet for each. Make copies of the worksheet, or put the information on separate blank sheets if you have had more than two jobs. No job is too small or pays too little. Employers are interested in what you can do. All your experiences can help prove you are a good worker.

Volunteer/Paid Work Experience Worksheet

Organization: ____

Street Address: ____

City/State/Province/Zip: ________________________________

Phone: (   ) ____

Supervisor or person in charge: __________________________

Starting Date: ________________ Ending Date: ________________

Starting Salary: ________________ Ending Salary: ________________

Job Title: ____

Any raises or promotions you received: ____________________

____

Other recognition (such as positive evaluations) you received: ____________

____

____

Reasons for leaving the job: ______________________________

List your job duties and responsibilities: ____________________

____

____

____

List any tools and equipment used: __________________________

____

____

____

List the self-management and transferable skills needed for the job: __________

____

____

List any special job-related skills or knowledge you need for the job: __________

____

____

What did you do well on this job; what were your accomplishments or results? ________

____

____

Volunteer/Paid Work Experience Worksheet

Organization: ____________________

Street Address: ____________________

City/State/Province/Zip: ____________________

Phone: ( ) ____________________

Supervisor or person in charge: ____________________

Starting Date: __________ Ending Date: __________

Starting Salary: __________ Ending Salary: __________

Job Title: ____________________

Any raises or promotions you received: ____________________

____

Other recognition (such as positive evaluations) you received: ____________________

____

____

Reasons for leaving the job: ____________________

List your job duties and responsibilities: ____________________

____

____

____

List any tools and equipment used: ____________________

____

____

____

List the self-management and transferable skills needed for the job: ____________________

____

____

List any special job-related skills or knowledge you need for the job: ____________________

____

____

What did you do well on this job; what were your accomplishments or results? ____________________

____

____

ACTIVITY School Experiences

A large part of your life experience comes from school. Since employers will be interested in this experience, use it to support your ability to do the job.

Vocational Courses

1. Have you taken any vocational courses? If yes, what types of jobs were they geared toward?

2. Vocational course titles:

3. What tools and equipment did you learn to use?

4. List the more important things you learned to do in these courses.

5. In these courses, what things do you feel you did best?

Other Courses

Name other courses you took that might be important in your next job.

Extracurricular Activities

Participation in sports, clubs and other extracurricular activities can help show that you are a hard worker or have other skills. Make a list of all the extracurricular activities that you have been involved in.

____

____

____

____

Select two or more of these activities, and complete the following form for them. If you want to include more than two extracurricular activities, make copies of the form or put the information on blank sheets of paper.

Extracurricular Activity Worksheet

Activity: ______________________________

____

____

How many months or years involved? ______________________________

Describe what you did in this activity: ______________________________

____

____

Self-management skills needed: ______________________________

____

____

Other skills you used or developed: ______________________________

____

____

Things you liked best about this activity: ______________________________

____

____

Explain how this activity prepared you to do well in the work world: ______________________________

____

____

Extracurricular Activity Worksheet

Activity: ____

____

____

How many months or years involved? ______________________

Describe what you did in this activity: ______________________

____

____

Self-management skills needed: ______________________

____

____

Other skills you used or developed: ______________________

____

____

Things you liked best about this activity: ______________________

____

____

Explain how this activity prepared you to do well in the work world: ______________________

____

____

ACTIVITY Hobbies, Family Activities, And Other Non-Work Experiences

Employers look for people who show an early interest in what they later want to do as a job. Things you do at home and outside of school show that you have experience or a special interest in something.

You may not think some of these things can "count" as experience, but many employers will. These things can be even more important to you if you have little paid work experience.

Think about the things you have done at home and outside of school that required responsibility, hard work, special knowledge, or that you feel you did well. List these below.

____

____

____

____

Select two or more of these experiences. For each, answer the questions below. If you want to include more than two, make extra copies of this form, or use blank sheets of paper.

Personal Development Experience Worksheet

Activity: ______________________________

____

____

____

How many months or years involved? ______________________________

____

Describe what you did in this activity: ______________________________

____

____

____

Things you liked best about this activity: ______________________________

____

____

____

Describe the skills you learned and used in this activity: ______________________________

____

____

____

Explain how this activity prepared you to do well in the work world: ______________________________

____

____

____

Personal Development Experience Worksheet

Activity: ____

____

____

____

How many months or years involved? ______________________

____

Describe what you did in this activity: ______________________

____

____

____

Things you liked best about this activity: ______________________

____

____

____

Describe the skills you learned and used in this activity: ______________

____

____

____

Explain how this activity prepared you to do well in the work world: __________

____

____

____

ACTIVITY Selecting Your References

Many employers want to verify the things you have told them about yourself. They will ask you for the names of people who know you and your work. Here are the sources of the most common references.

Work References

This is usually the person who supervised you on a paid or volunteer job. Most employers think that these are the best sources of information for determining the kind of worker you are.

Personal And Professional References

These include people who know you well. Most employers will not bother to contact a relative or friend about you. They know that these people like you but may not be able to give them information about your work skills.

Better choices are teachers, coaches, scout leaders, and other adults who know you well. These are people who can tell an employer that you are likely to make a good worker.

Remember

Pick references who will say good things about you. Talk to them in advance, and discuss what they will say. Tell them the type of job you are looking for and the skills and experience you have to do it well. Make sure these people can be reached easily by phone during the day. This is when most employers will call.

Your instructor will give you directions on completing the worksheet that follows.

Work and Personal References Worksheet

In the spaces below, list the persons you might use as your work and personal references. The *Data Minder* will provide additional information on these references.

Work References

Name: ______________________

Position: ______________________

Phone: (   ) ______________________

Place of employment: ______________________

Name: ______________________

Position: ______________________

Phone: (   ) ______________________

Place of employment: ______________________

Name: ______________________

Position: ______________________

Phone: (   ) ______________________

Place of employment: ______________________

Name: ______________________

Position: ______________________

Phone: (   ) ______________________

Place of employment: ______________________

Personal References

Name: ______________________

Relationship: ______________________

Phone: (   ) ______________________

Name: ______________________

Relationship: ______________________

Phone: (   ) ______________________

Name: ______________________

Relationship: ______________________

Phone: (   ) ______________________

Name: ______________________

Relationship: ______________________

Phone: (   ) ______________________

ACTIVITY The *Data Minder:* A Portable Job Search Assistant

The *Data Minder* is a booklet that is bound into the back of this book. It is designed to help you remember the many details that will be asked of you throughout the job search — such as phone numbers, dates, addresses, and other information.

Once it is completed, you can carry the *Data Minder* with you throughout your job search. It will help you complete applications, answer interview questions and help you remember key points covered throughout this course.

Follow your teacher's instructions in completing the *Data Minder*. Note that some of the content can not be completed until you have covered this material later in this book.

CONTINUED FROM PAGE 22

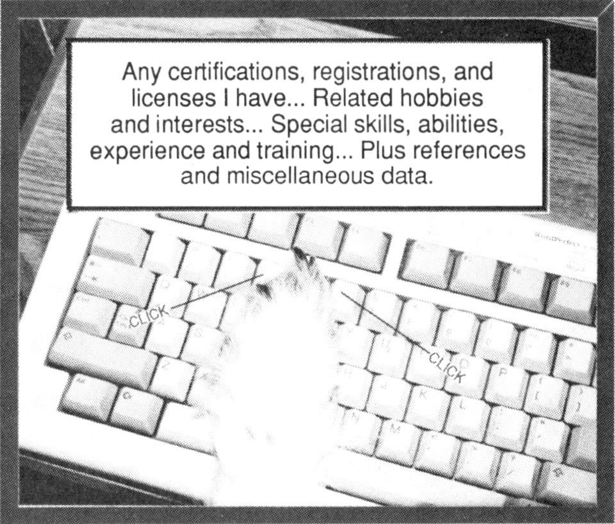

CRISIS HOT LINE

featuring Emma Lemming

CHAPTER 5

AVOID THE APPLICATION TRAP

*Many people think that filling out an application is the same as applying for a job. But it isn't! Most employers use applications to screen people **out**, not in. If your application is messy, incomplete, or shows you do not have the "right" experience or training, you probably will not get an interview.*

Though many smaller employers don't use applications, you will often be asked to fill out an application during your job search. For this reason it is important to know how to complete them properly.

Tips—Completing The Application

Use the following tips as a guideline when filling out a job application to increase your chances for an actual job interview.

- **Follow instructions.** Read all instructions carefully before completing each section.
- **Be neat.** Print clearly, and avoid cross-outs and erasures as much as possible.
- **Avoid negatives.** Remember that employers will use anything negative as a reason to screen you out. It is often better to leave a section blank than to provide negative information. If it comes up in an interview, you can explain it then.
- **Emphasize your skills and accomplishments.** Find a way to mention your strengths, even if the application does not specifically ask for them. Mention your most important self-management and transferable skills. The education, vocational training, and work experience sections are often good places to mention strengths. If you are short on paid work experience, mention your volunteer work and related hobbies under the experience section.
- **If a section does not apply to you.** Write "N.A." (not applicable) or a dash to show that you have read that item but that it does not apply to you.
- **Use an erasable black pen.** Completing your application with a black erasable pen will allow you to make neat corrections and give it a professional look.

ACTIVITY An Introduction To Albert C. Smith

Seeing someone else make mistakes on completing a job application can help you avoid the same mistakes. Meet "Albert C. Smith." Like many of you, he also wanted to find a job. This activity shows you an application Albert completed at a Department Store. It is reproduced on the next two pages.

I am sure you will agree that Albert could have done a better job in completing his application. Your job is to review Albert's application and circle the mistakes he made. There are over 30 mistakes in this application. See how many of them you can find!

Please Turn To The Next Page—Albert's Application

APPLICATION FOR EMPLOYMENT

PLEASE PRINT INFORMATION REQUESTED IN INK.

Date April 1

BROWN'S IS AN EQUAL OPPORTUNITY EMPLOYER and fully subscribes to the principles of Equal Employment Opportunity. Brown's has adopted an Affirmative Action Program to ensure that all applicants and employees are considered for hire, promotion and, job status, without regard to race, color, religion, sex, national origin, age, handicap, or status as a disabled veteran or veteran of the Vietnam Era.

To protect the interests of all concerned, applicants for certain job assignments must pass a physical examination before they are hired.

Note: This application will be considered active for 90 days. If you have not been employed within this period and are still interested in employment at Brown's, please contact the office where you applied and request that your application be reactivated.

Name Albert C. Smith (Last / First / Middle)   Social Security Number 411-~~40~~ 76-2614 (Please present your Social Security Card for review.)

Address 1526 N. Otter (Number / Street / City / State / Zip Code)

County Marion   Current phone or nearest phone ______

Previous Address Same (Number / Street / City / State / Zip Code)   Best time of day to contact any

(Answer only if position for which you are applying requires driving.)

If hired, can you furnish proof of age? Yes ☒ No ☐   Licensed to drive car? ☐ YES ☐ NO

If hired, can you furnish proof that you are legally entitled to work in U.S.? Yes ☒ No ☐   Is license valid in this state? ☐ YES ☐ NO

Have you ever been employed by Brown's? Yes ______ No X If so, when ______ Position ______

Have you a relative in the employ of Brown's Department store? Yes ______ No X

A PHYSICAL OR MENTAL DISABILITY WILL NOT CAUSE REJECTION IF IN BROWN'S MEDICAL OPINION YOU ARE ABLE TO SATISFACTORILY PERFORM IN THE POSITION FOR WHICH YOU ARE BEING CONSIDERED. Alternative placement, if available, of an applicant who does not meet the physical standards of the job for which he/she was originally considered is permitted.

Do you have any physical or mental impairment which may limit your ability to perform the job for which you are applying? Yes, Have a back problem and was in Central State for 6 months

If yes, what can reasonably be done to accommodate your limitation? ______

EDUCATION

School Attended	No. of Years	Name of School	City/State	Graduate?	Course or College Major	Average Grades
Grammar	6	Holy Trinity	Scranton	Yes	General	B
Jr. High	3	Crestview	" "	"	" "	B
Sr. High	3	WCHS	" "	"	College Prep	C
Other						
College	3	State U	Scranton	NO	Degree	C

MILITARY SERVICE

BRANCH OF SERVICE	DATE ENTERED SERVICE*	DATE OF DISCHARGE*	HIGHEST RANK HELD	SERVICE-RELATED SKILLS AND EXPERIENCE APPLICABLE TO CIVILIAN EMPLOYMENT
USA	1984	1986	E-2	~~[illegible]~~ radio

***Do not complete if applying in the state of California.**

What experience or training have you had other than your work experience, military service and education? (Community activities, hobbies, etc.)

I am interested in the type of work I have checked:

Sales X Office X Mechanical X Warehouse X Other (Specify) X

Or the following specific Job Anything

I am seeking (check only one):

- X Temporary employment (6 days or less)
- X Seasonal employment (one season, e.g. Christmas)
- X Regular employment (employment for indefinite period of time)

If temporary, indicate dates available ______

I am available for (check only one): Work

- ☒ Part-Time
- ☒ Full-Time

If part-time, indicate maximum hours per week ______, and enter hours available in block to the right.

HOURS AVAILABLE FOR WORK	
Sun.	To
Mon.	To
Tues.	To
Wed.	To
Thurs.	To
Fri.	To
Sat.	To

(Written across the block: Any time)

Have you been convicted during the past seven years of a serious crime involving a person's life or property?

NO ☒ YES ☒ If yes, explain. ~~drunk in public~~

REFERENCES

LIST BELOW YOUR FOUR MOST RECENT EMPLOYERS, BEGINNING WITH THE CURRENT OR MOST RECENT ONE: IF YOU HAVE HAD LESS THAN FOUR EMPLOYERS, USE THE REMAINING SPACES FOR PERSONAL REFERENCES. IF YOU WERE EMPLOYED UNDER A MAIDEN OR OTHER NAME, PLEASE ENTER THAT NAME IN THE RIGHT HAND MARGIN. IF APPLICABLE, ENTER SERVICE IN THE ARMED FORCES ON THE REVERSE SIDE.

NAMES AND ADDRESSES OF FORMER EMPLOYERS, BEGINNING WITH THE CURRENT OR MOST RECENT	Nature of Employer's Business	Name of your Supervisor	What kind of work did you do?	Starting Date	Starting Pay	Date of Leaving	Pay at Leaving	Why did you leave? Give details
NOTE: State reason for and length of inactivity between present application date and last employer								
Name SPS; Address Walnut St; Tel. No.; City Scranton; State PA; Zip Code	School	Ernie Burgess	clean up	Month ?; Year 86	$6.00 an hr. Per Week	Month 3; Year 87	$6.00 Per Week	Fired
NOTE: State reason for and length of inactivity between last employer and second last employer. Looked for a job - almost a year								
Name Fred Willis; Address ?; Tel. No. ?; City Scranton; State PA; Zip Code	Houses	Rafael	electrician's helper & labor	Month 8; Year 87	$7.00 an hour Per Week	Month 10; Year [illegible]	$7.00 Per Week	Boss always picked on me
NOTE: State reason for and length of inactivity between second last employer and third last employer. Looked for a job								
Name Wayne Const.; Address 1430 N. Anderson; Tel. No. 555-4141; City Scranton; State PA; Zip Code	construction	Mark Lenski	Jack Hammer & wiring	Month 6; Year 83	$5.75 Per Week	Month 4; Year 84	$6.00 Per Week	company went broke
NOTE: State reason for and length of inactivity between third last employer and fourth last employer. unable to find work								
Name Central State Hosp; Address Washington St; Tel. No.; City Scranton; State PA; Zip Code	mental hospital	Lynn Donovan	clean up	Month ?; Year 86	$1.20 an hour Per Week	Month 7; Year 86	$1.20 Per Week	I got better and was discharged

I certify that the information in this application is correct to the best of my knowledge and understand that any misstatement or omission of information is grounds for dismissal in accordance with Brown's policy. I authorize the references listed above to give you any and all information concerning my previous employment and any pertinent information they may have, personal or otherwise, and release all parties from all liability for any damage that may result form furnishing same to you. In consideration of my employment, I agree to conform to the rules and regulations of Browns, and my employment and compensation can be terminated with or without cause, and with or without notice, at any time, at the option of either the Company or myself. I understand that no unit manager or representative of Brown's other than the President or Vice-President of the Company, has any authority to enter into any agreement for employment for any specified period of time, or to make any agreement contrary to the foregoing. In some states, the law requires that Brown's have my written permission before obtaining consumer reports on me, and I hereby authorize Brown's to obtain such reports.

Applicant's Signature Smith, Albert C.

NOT TO BE FILLED OUT BY APPLICANT

INTERVIEWER'S COMMENTS		
	Date of Emp.	
	Dept. or Div.	Regular ☐ Part-Time ☐
	Job Title	
	Job Title Code	Job Grade
	Compensation Arrangement	
Prospect for	Manager Approving	
1. / 2.	Employee No.	Rack No.

Tested	(Store will enter dates as required.)		Mailed	Completed
Physical examination scheduled for		REFERENCE REQUESTS		
Physical examination form completed		CONSUMER REPORT		
		With. Tax (W-4)		
		State With. Tax		
Review Card prepared	Minor's Work Permit			
Timecard prepared	Proof of Birth			
	Training Material Given to Employee			

Unit Name and Number Albert Smith

ACTIVITY Completing A Sample Job Application

After you have found and discussed the errors in Albert's application, you are ready to complete an application yourself. In completing your own application, be as neat and as thorough as possible. You have already gathered much of the information you need in earlier chapters. Refer to them as needed.

Few applications are as thorough as the sample application you are about to complete. This application is actually used by a large company. It will prepare you to answer the questions on most real applications. Be neat, complete all sections accurately, and act as if you were completing it to get the job you really want.

Good luck!

Personal Qualifications Statement

Read instructions before completing form

1. Kind of position *(job)* you are filing for *(or title and number of announcement)*

2. Options for which you wish to be considered *(if listed in the announcment)*

3. Home phone — Area Code | Number

4. Work phone — Area Code | Number | Extension

5. Sex *(for statistics only)* ☐ Male ☐ Female

6. Other last names ever used.

7. Name *(Last, First, Middle)*

Street address or RFD no. *(include apartment no., if any)*

City | State | ZIP Code

8. Birthplace *(City & State, or foreign country)*

9. Birth date *(Month, day, year)*

10. Social Security Number

11. If you have ever been employed by the Federal Government as a civilian, give your highest grade, classification series, and job title.

Dates of service in highest grade *(Month, day, and year)*

From — To

12. If you currently have an application on file with the Office of Personnel Management for appointment to a Federal position, list, (a) the name of the area office maintaining your application, (b) the position for which you filed, and *(if appropriate)* (c) the date of your notice of rating, (d) your identification number, and (e) your rating.

13. Lowest pay or grade you will accept.

PAY		GRADE
$ per	OR	

14. When will you be available for work? *(Month, and year)*

DO NOT WRITE IN THIS BLOCK
FOR USE OF EXAMINING OFFICE ONLY

Material ☐ Submitted ☐ Returned — Entered register

Notations:

Form reviewed:

Form approved:

ANNOUNCEMENT NO.

Option	Grade	Earned Rating	Preference	Aug. Rating
			☐ 5-Points (Tent.)	
			☐ 10 Pts. 30% or More Comp. Dis.	
			☐ 10 Pts. Less Than 30% Comp. Dis.	
			☐ Other 10 Points	
			☐ Disallowed	
Initials and date			☐ Being Investigated	

STATEMENT NO.

THIS SPACE FOR USE OF APPOINTING OFFICER ONLY

Preference has been verified through proof that the separation was under honorable conditions, and other proof as required.

☐ 5-Point ☐ 10-Points 30% or More Compensable Disability ☐ 10 Points Less Than 30% Compensable Disability ☐ 10-Point Other

Signature and title

Agency | Date

15. Are you available for temporary employment lasting:

(Acceptance or refusal of temporary employment will not affect your consideration for other appointments.)

	YES	NO
A. Less than 1 month?		
B. 1 to 4 months?		
C. 5 to 12 months?		

16. Are you interested in being considered for employment by:

	YES	NO
A. State and local government agencies?		
B. Congressional and other public offices?		
C. Public international organizations?		

17. Where will you accept a job?

	YES	NO
A. In the Washington, D.C. Metropolitan area?		
B. Outside the 50 United States?		
C. Anyplace in the United States?		
D. Only in *(specify locality)*		

18. Indicate your availability for overnight travel:

A. Not available for overnight travel	
B. 1 to 5 nights per month	
C. 6 to 10 nights per month	
D. 11 or more nights per month	

19. Are you available for part-time positions *(fewer than 40 hours per week)* offering:

	YES	NO
A. 20 or fewer hours per week?		
B. 21 to 31 hours per week?		
C. 32 to 39 hours per week?		

20. Veteran Preference. Answer all parts. If a part does not apply to you, answer "NO". (YES / NO)

A. Have you ever served on active duty in the United States military service? *(Exclude tours of active duty for training in Reserves or National Guard)*.

B. Have you ever been discharged from the armed services under other than honorable conditions? You may omit any such discharge changed to honorable or general by a Discharge Review Board or similar authority). If "YES", give details in item 34.

C. Do you claim 5-point preference based on active duty in the armed forces? If "YES", you will be required to furnish records to support your claim at the time you are appointed.

D. Do you claim 10-point preference? If "YES", check the type of preference claimed and complete and attach Standard Form 15, "Claim for 10-Point Veteran Preference," together with the proof requested in that form.

Type of Preference: ☐ Compensable Disability 30% or More ☐ Compensable Disability Below 30% ☐ Non-compensable Disability ☐ Purple Heart Recipient ☐ Spouse ☐ Widow(er) ☐ Mother

E. List dates, branch, and serial number of all active service *(enter "N/A", if not applicable)*

From	To	Branch of Service	Serial or Service Number

(Continued on next page)

21. Experience. Begin with current or most recent job or volunteer experience and work back. Account for periods of unemployment exceeding three months and your residence address at that time on the last line of the experience blocks in order of occurrence.

May inquiry be made of your present employer regarding your character qualifications, and record of employment? *(A "NO" will not affect your consideration for employment opportunities except for Administrative Law Judge positions.)* ☐ YES ☐ NO

A

Name and address of employer's organization *(include ZIP Code, if known)*		Dates employed *(give months and year)* From To	Average number of hours per week
		Salary or earnings Beginning $ per Ending $ per	Place of employment City State
Exact title of your position	Name of immediate supervisor	Area Code Telephone number	Number and kind of employees you supervise
Kind of business or organization *(manufacturing, accounting, social services, etc)*	If Federal service, civilian or military, series, grade or rank, and date of last promotion.		Your reason for wanting to leave
Description of work *(Describe your specific duties, responsibilities and accomplishments in this job)*			
			For agency use *(skill codes, etc.)*

B

Name and address of employer's organization *(include ZIP code, if known)*		Dates employed *(give month and year)* From To	Average number of hours per week
		Salary or earnings Beginning $ per Ending $ per	Place of employment City State
Exact title of your position	Name of immediate supervisor	Area Code Telephone number	Number and kind of employees you supervised
Kind of business or organization *(manufacturing, accounting, social services, etc.)*	If Federal service, civilian or military series, grade or rank, and date of last promotion		Your reason for leaving
Description of work *(Describe your specific duties, responsibilities and accomplishments in this job)*			
			For agency use *(skill codes, etc.)*

C

Name and address of employer's organization *(include ZIP code, if known)*		Dates employed *(give month and year)* From To	Average number of hours per week
		Salary or earnings Beginning $ per Ending $ per	Place of employment City State
Exact title of your position	Name of immediate supervisor	Area Code Telephone number	Number and kind of employees you supervised
Kind of business or organization *(manufacturing, accounting, social services, etc.)*	If Federal service, civilian or military series, grade or rank, and date of last promotion		Your reason for leaving
Description of work *(Describe your specific duties, responsibilities and accomplishments in this job)*			
			For agency use *(skill codes, etc.)*

22. A. Special qualifications and skills *(skills with machines, patents or inventions, your most important publications [do not submit copies unless requested]; your public speaking and publications experience, membership in professional or scientific societies, etc.)*

B. Kind of license or certificate *(pilot, registered nurse, lawyer, radio operator, CPA, etc.)*	C. Latest license or certificate		D. Approximate number of words per minute	
	Year	State or other licensing authority	Typing	Shorthand

23. A. Did you graduate from high school or will you graduate within the next nine months, or do you have a GED high school equivalency certificate?

Yes	Month and Year	No	Highest grade completed

B. Name and location *(city and State)* of latest high school attended

C. Name and location *(city, State, and ZIP Code, if known)* of college or university. *(If you expect to graduate within nine months, give MONTH and YEAR you expect to receive your degree.)*	Dates Attended		Years Completed		No. of Credits Completed		Type of Degree *(e.g., B.A.)*	Year of Degree
	From	To	Day	Night	Semester Hours	Quarter Hours		

D. Chief undergraduate college subjects	No. of Credits Completed		E. Chief graduate college subjects	No. of Credits Completed	
	Semester Hours	Quarter Hours		Semester Hours	Quarter Hours

F. Major field of study at highest level of college work		

G. Other schools or training *(for example, trade, vocational, Armed Forces or business)*. Give for each the name and location *(city, State and ZIP Code, if known)* of school, dates attended, subjects studied, number of classroom hours of instruction per week, certificate, and any other pertinent data.

24. Honors, awards, and fellowships received

25. Languages other than English. List the languages *(other than English)* in which you are proficient and indicate your level of proficiency by putting a check mark (✓) in the appropriate columns. **Candidates for positions requiring conversational ability in a language other than English may be given an interview conducted solely in that language.** Describe in item 34 how you gained your language skills and the amount of experience you have had *(e.g., completed 72 hours of classroom training, spoke language at home for 18 years, self-taught, etc.)*.

Name of Language(s)	PROFICIENCY							
	Can Prepare and Deliver Lectures		Can Converse		Have Facility to Translate Articles, Technical Materials, etc.		Can Read Articles, Technical Materials, etc., for Own Use	
	Fluently	With Difficulty	Fluently	Passably	Into English	From English	Easily	With Difficulty

26. References: List three persons who are NOT related to you and who have definite knowledge of your qualifications and fitness for the position for which you are applying. Do not repeat names of supervisors listed under Item 21, Experience.

Full Name	Present Business or Home Address *(Number, Street, City, State and ZIP Code)*	Telephone Number *(Include Area Code)*	Business or Occupation

Answer Items 27 through 33 by placing an "X" in the proper column	YES	NO
27. Are you a citizen of the United States? If "NO", give country of which you are a citizen		
NOTE: A conviction or a firing does not necessarily mean you cannot be appointed. The circumstances of the occurrence(s) and how long ago it (they) occurred are important. Give all the facts so that a decision can be made. 28. Within the last five years have you been fired from any job for any reason?		
29. Within the last five years have you quit a job after being notified that you would be fired? If your answer to 28 or 29 is "YES" give details in Item 34. Show the name and address *(including ZIP Code)* of employer, approximate date, and reasons in each case. This information should agree with your answers in Item 21. Experience.		
30. A. Have you **ever** been convicted, forfeited collateral, or are you now under charges for **any felony** or **any** firearms or explosives offense against the law? *(A felony is defined as any offense punishable by imprisonment for a term exceeding one year, but does not include any offense classified under the laws of a State as a misdemeanor which is punishable by a term of imprisonment of two years or less)*		
B. During the past seven years have you been convicted, imprisoned, on probation or parole or forfeited collateral, or are you now under charges for any offense against the law not included in A above?		
NOTE: When answering A and B above, you may omit (1) traffic fines for which you paid a fine of $50.00 or less, (2) any offense committed before your 18th birthday which was finally adjudicated in a juvenile court or under a youth offender law: (3) any conviction the record of which has been expunged under Federal or State law; and (4) any conviction set aside under the Federal Youth Corrections Act or similar State authority		
31. While in the military service were you ever convicted by a general court-martial? If your answer to 30A, 30B, or 31 is "YES", give details in Item 34. Show for each offense; (1) date; (2) charge; (3) place; (4) court; and (5) action taken.		
32. Does the United States Government employ in a civilian capacity or as a member of the Armed Forces any relative of yours *(by blood or marriage)? (See Item 32 in the attached instruction sheet)* *If your answer to 32 is "YES", give in Item 34 for such relatives: (1) name, (2) present address (including ZIP Code)*; (3) relationship, (4) department, agency, or branch of the armed forces.		
33. Do you receive, or do you have pending, application for retirement or retainer pay, pension, or other compensation based upon military. Federal civilian, or District of Columbia Government service? If your answer to 33 is "YES", give details in Item 34. If military retired pay, include the rank at which you retired.		

Your Statement cannot be processed until you have answered all questions, including Items 27 through 33 above.
Be sure you have placed an "X" to the left of EVERY marker (◄) above, either in the "YES" or "NO" column.

34, Item No.	Space for detailed answers. Indicate Item numbers to which the answers apply.

If more space is required, use full sheets of paper approximately the same size at this page. Write on each sheet your name, birth date, and announcement or position title. Attach all sheets to this Statement at the top of page 3.

ATTENTION—THIS STATEMENT MUST BE SIGNED

Read the following paragraphs carefully before signing this Statement

A false answer to any question in this Statement may be grounds for not employing you, or for dismissing you after you begin work, and may be punishable by fine or imprisonment (U.S. Code, Title 18, Section 1001). All the information you give will be considered in reviewing your Statement.

AUTHORITY FOR RELEASE OF INFORMATION

I have completed this Statement with the knowledge and understanding that any or all items contained herein may be subject to investigation prescribed by law or Presidential directive and I consent to the release of information concerning my capacity and fitness by employers, educational institutions, law enforcement agencies, and other individuals and agencies, to duly accredited investigators, Personnel Staffing Specialists, and other authorized employees of the Federal Government for that purpose.

CERTIFICATION	SIGNATURE *(sign in ink)*	DATE
I certify that all of the statements made by me are true, complete and correct to the best of my knowledge and belief, and are in made in good faith.		

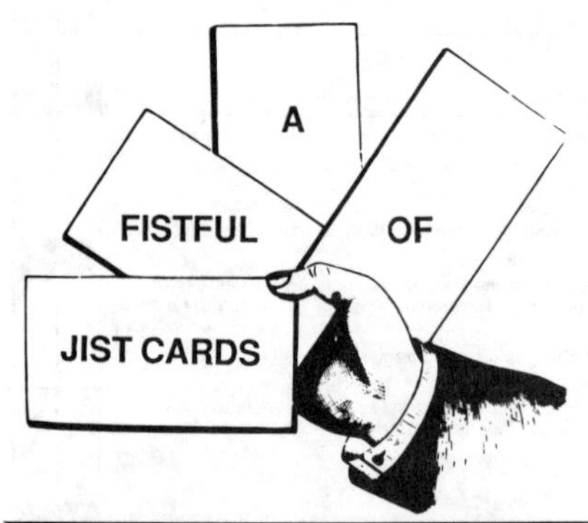

In preceding chapters, you've been given some clues about what JIST Cards are. Have you been perceptive? Well, now is the time to test your mental mettle. See if you can find the JIST Card in this **JIST INTELLIGENCE TEST!**

1

❑ YES ❑ NO

2

❑ YES ❑ NO

3

❑ YES ❑ NO

4

❑ YES ❑ NO

5

❑ YES ❑ NO

6

Thomas A. Watson

Home phone: *(to be invented)*
Work phone: *(to be invented)*

Position Desired: Inventor's Assistant

Skills: Over 5 years of experience with tin-can and taut-string communication systems. Knowledgeable in both theoretical and applied scientific principles pertaining to mechanical and electromechanical devices. Can install land lines, fabricate prototype equipment, jury-rig induction coils, recharge lead-acid batteries, and perform general shop maintenance. Experienced in solving design, development, and modification problems.

Willing to work any shift.

Reliable, Inventive, Hard-working, and a real Go-getter.

❑ YES ❑ NO

COMPARE YOUR SELECTIONS WITH THE ANSWERS LISTED ON PAGE 51.

CHAPTER 6

JIST CARDS: A MINI-RESUME

*In this chapter, you will create your own **JIST Card**. You will learn the anatomy of a **JIST Card** by analyzing its different parts, the effective uses of the **JIST Card** in your job search, and the construction of your own **JIST Card**.*

The Mini-Resume

A *JIST Card* is a mini-resume that can be used in many ways during your job search. Although it is only 3" × 5", your *JIST Card* will include the information most employers need to know.

Read the sample *JIST Card* below. Imagine that you are an employer who hires people with similar skills. Your "company" may or may not have a job opening at this time. Review the information on the card and let yourself react naturally to what you feel about this potential employee.

John Kijek

Home: (219) 232-9213
Message: (219) 637-6643

Position Desired: Auto Mechanic

Skills: Over three years' work experience, including one year in a full-time training program. Familiar with all hand tools and basic diagnostic equipment. Can handle common repairs such as tune-ups, brakes, exhaust systems, electrical and mechanical repairs. Am a fast worker, often completing jobs in less than standard time. Have all tools and can start work immediately.

Prefer full-time work, any shift.

Honest, reliable, good with people.

What Do You Think?

If you were an employer, how would you feel about the person whose *JIST Card* you just read?

____

____

____

____

____

____

Would you interview this person if you had an opening?__________________

Even though it appears to give very little information, most employers feel positive about *JIST Cards*. Many would give an interview if they had an opening. They are that impressed!

Some Ways You Can Use A *JIST Card*

- Attach one to your application or resume.
- Present one as your business card before or after an interview.
- Leave one with your references.
- Give several to each of your friends, relatives, and others who might help you in your job search. (Ask them to pass them on to others who might know of an opening!)
- Leave one with employers when you are refused an application or an interview. (It could help them change their minds!)
- Enclose one in a thank-you note following an interview or with other job search correspondence.

Write any other ideas for the uses of your *JIST Card* here:

____

____

____

____

____

____

____

Helpful Hint

At the beginning of this course, you identified the self-management, transferable, and job-related skills that you felt were your best and supported each one with an example. These skills and examples will be used in developing your own *JIST Card.*

The Anatomy Of A *JIST Card*

JIST Cards are more complicated than they first appear. Look over the various parts of a *JIST Card* in the following sample. It will help you learn how to create your own card.

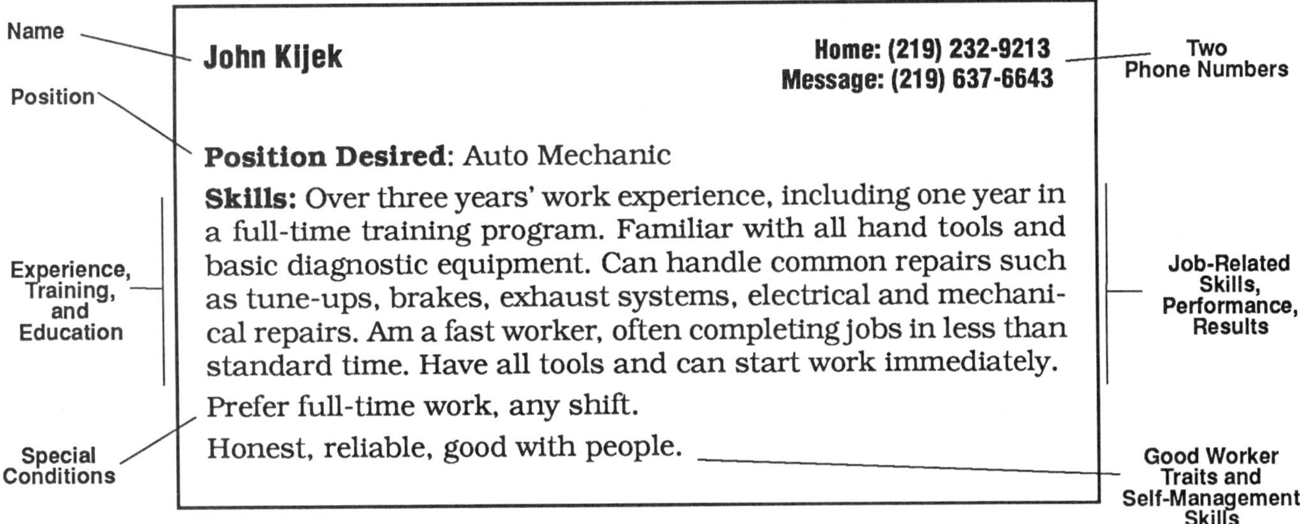

3" × 5" Pastel Card

Tips—Creating Your Own *JIST Card*

- **Name.** Use your name as it is spoken. Avoid nicknames.
- **Phone Number.** An employer will almost always try to contact you by phone. If your home phone is not always answered during the day (or if you don't have one), ask a reliable friend or relative to take messages. Many *JIST Cards* include a second phone number to increase the chance of an employer reaching you.
- **Position/Job Objective.** If your job objective is too specific, it will limit the jobs for which you may be considered. Instead, use a job objective that allows you to be considered for more positions but is not *too* general.
- **Skills.** This section is actually made up of several parts.

  a. *Education & Experience.* Take credit for everything you've done! Everything can count, including education, plus paid employment, plus related volunteer work, hobbies, and other informal experience. Use the following formula to figure your total length of experience. Then list your total experience as well as any special training, certificates, or achievements.

Experience	**Months/Years**
1. Total time worked in similar jobs.	________
2. Total time worked in other jobs.	________
3. Total time informal/volunteer work and related hobbies.	________
4. Total time in related training and education	________
TOTAL Experience/Time (add 1 + 2 + 3 + 4)	________

b. *Job-Related Skills.* Mention the things you can do specific to the job such as using special tools and equipment, knowing procedures, having special job-related skills. Emphasize accomplishments, and use numbers (such as percentage of sales or profits increased, number of units produced, etc.).

c. *Transferable Skills.* Mention ones that are important to the job *and* that you do well. Refer to the skills checklists in Chapter 3. Use examples where possible.

- **Special Conditions.** This is an optional section. Use it to list any special advantages you offer to an employer that don't fit elsewhere.
- **Self-Management Skills.** Include at least three of your strongest self-management skills. Select the ones from your checklist in Chapter 3 that seem important for this job.

Sample *JIST Cards*

Look over the sample *JIST Cards* that follow for ideas for your own.

Sandy Zaremba

Home: (219) 232-7608
Message: (219) 234-7465

Position: General Office/Clerical

Over two years work experience plus one year of training in office practices. Type 55 wpm, trained in word processing operations, post general ledger, handle payables, receivables, and most accounting tasks. Responsible for daily deposits averaging $5,000 weekly. Good interpersonal skills. Can meet strict deadlines and handle pressure well.

Willing to work any hours.

Organized, honest, reliable, and hard working.

THOMAS WELBORN

Home: (602) 253-9678
Message: (602) 257-6643

Objective: Electronics—installation, maintenance and sales

Skills: Four years work experience plus two years advanced training in electronics. A.S. degree in Electronics Engineering Technology. Managed a $300,000/yr. business while going to school full time, with grades in the top 25%. Familiar with all major electronic diagnostic and repair equipment. Hands-on experience with medical, consumer, communications, and industrial electronics equipment and applications. Good problem-solving and communication skills. Customer service oriented.

Willing to do what it takes to get the job done.

Learn quickly, meet deadlines, cooperative.

ACTIVITY Practice *JIST Card*

Use the following form to write up a first draft of your *JIST Card*. You may want to make rough drafts on separate sheets of paper for some sections of the form. When your information is "right," you can then transfer the material to this form.

JIST Card First Draft Worksheet

Name: ______________________________

Home Phone: ______________________________

Message Phone: ______________________________

Position Desired: ______________________________

____

Education & Training: ______________________________

____

____

____

Job-related skills statement: ______________________________

____

____

____

____

____

Transferable skills statement: ______________________________

____

____

____

____

____

Special conditions (Optional): ______________________________

____

Good Worker Traits/Self-Management Skills: ______________________________

____

____

Now use the information from above to write out a complete *JIST Card* in the spaces that follow:

JIST Card Final Draft Worksheet

Name:____________________ Phone:____________________

Alternate Phone:____________________

Position Desired: ____________________

Skills

Experience, Training, & Education: ____________________

Job-Related, Performance & Results: ____________________

Transferable: ____________________

Special Conditions (Optional): ____________________

Good Worker Traits/Self-Management Skills: ____________________

Assignment

Complete your final *JIST Card* on a 3" × 5" index card, and hand it in for a graded assignment. It can be neatly hand printed for this assignment.

When you get your card back and make all necessary corrections, you should make arrangements to have it professionally printed. It will be more noticeable if your cards are printed on a soft, light color such as beige, cream, or gray.

You should consider having approximately 200-250 *JIST Cards* made. If so, make arrangements with the printer for you to see and approve the final draft before the printer completes your order.

Don't forget to write the content of your *JIST Card* in your *Data Minder* booklet!

OFFICIAL ANSWERS FOR THE JIST INTELLIGENCE TEST ON PAGE 44.

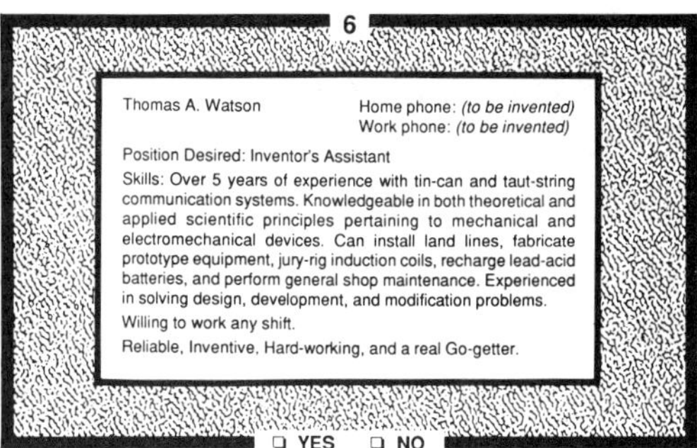
6

Thomas A. Watson — Home phone: *(to be invented)* Work phone: *(to be invented)*

Position Desired: Inventor's Assistant

Skills: Over 5 years of experience with tin-can and taut-string communication systems. Knowledgeable in both theoretical and applied scientific principles pertaining to mechanical and electromechanical devices. Can install land lines, fabricate prototype equipment, jury-rig induction coils, recharge lead-acid batteries, and perform general shop maintenance. Experienced in solving design, development, and modification problems.

Willing to work any shift.

Reliable, Inventive, Hard-working, and a real Go-getter.

YES NO

1. No, it's not a JIST Card. This is an old "Hire Me" vest, predecessor to the modern "Hire Me" T-shirt. When first marketed in early April 1886, this vest was touted as being very cost- efficient since as many as 15 job seekers could share in its expense and, then, simultaneously advertise themselves to employers. (This gave rise to the expression "vested interest.") Since no employer ever took interest in any person or persons wearing one, the vest was pulled off the market by mid-April 1886.

2. No, this is not a JIST Card. It's a variation (90-degree vertical rotation) on the traditional sandwich board. This method of job seeking was popular during the Great Depression. If a person had lost his or her shirt in the stock market crash, a sandwich board could hide the fact from potential employers. This method seldom led to employment however. And it never was regarded as a truly chic fashion statement.

3. Nope, it's not a JIST Card. This method would only help someone seeking a position as a DMDM (pronounced dum'-dum,' **D**emented **M**inor **D**rum **M**ajor). Be forewarned: Such positions are rare in the U.S. and the pay is usually limited to all the tossed salad one can catch!

4. No. You're getting warmer, but this is not a JIST Card.

5. No, No, No. Wearing elephant suits and/or carrying "Hire Me" carpetbags should only be performed by incumbent Republican politicians who are running uncontested campaigns for minor posts at the city or county level. (Even then, attorneys specializing in costume law should be consulted with regard to local statutes and state laws that may apply.)

6. YES, THIS IS A JIST CARD! See how well it presents a job seeker's Name, Phone Number, Job Objective, Skills, Special Conditions, and Self-Management Skills. Hey, the odds were 5 to 1 against you, but if you picked this one, consider yourself to be reasonably intelligent. Hotcha! And now that you've got your gray matter all warmed up, you might as well learn how to make and use your very own JIST Card. See page 47.

In our last episode, Theta's "Starr Shuttle" was shot down over the treacherous Want Ad Wasteland by those nefarious ne'er-do-wells, the Kut Bax. Narrowly averting her dance with death, Theta ejected into the Wasteland just nanoseconds before her spacecraft careened into the vast "Wage Slaves Wanted" sector. Now, after weeks of following the seemingly endless maze of dead-end trails, and nearing the last of her survival rations and strength, Theta stumbles into a clearing in the wilderness. Perhaps she has found her sanctuary. Or perhaps she should continue...

BEYOND WANT AD WASTELAND AND THE PLACEMENT MACHINES!

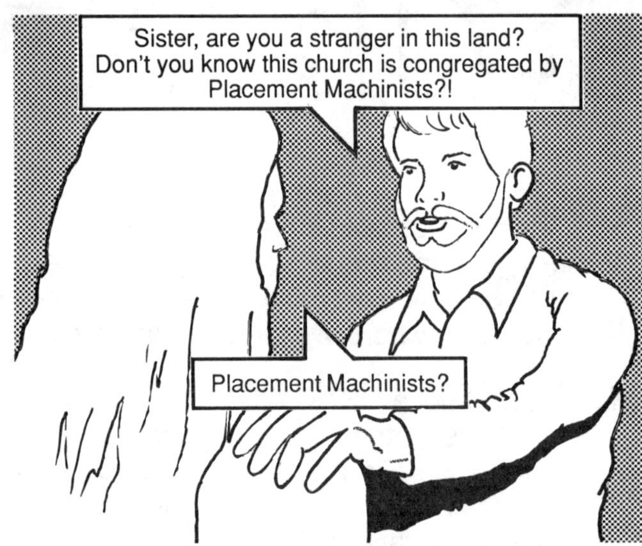

*Excerpt from "Brother Dave's Intro Hymn for the FIRST CHURCH OF THE ALL-DAY SEEKER Radio Hour"—with acknowledgments to P.T. Barnum for the first line and to W.C. Fields for the last. Music and lyrics by Bro. Dave.

CONTINUED ON PAGE 63

CHAPTER 7

FINDING JOB LEADS

*For some people, finding **a** job is not too hard. Many younger people can find lower paying, entry level jobs (in restaurants and fast food places for example) quite easily. But finding **the** job is often more difficult. The competition is greater. The more desirable jobs have more people with a wider range of experience competing for them. This chapter will give you information on various job search techniques that will help you get a competitive edge.*

Job Leads—The Hows, Whats, Whens, and Wheres

ACTIVITY How People Find Jobs

The major techniques people use to find jobs are listed below. Write in the percentage of job seekers you think actually found jobs using each technique. The total should be 100%.

1. From a lead they got from the help wanted ads. __________
2. Heard about the opening from people they knew. __________
3. Referred by the state employment service. __________
4. Referred by a private employment agency. __________
5. Contacted the employer directly. __________
6. Referred by school placement office. __________
7. Took civil service test. __________
8. Other methods. __________

Compare your guesses with others in the class, then look up the answers at the end of this chapter. Discuss your guesses and the actual figures in class.

Where To Find Job Leads

Most people are surprised to find that fewer than 15% of all job seekers get their jobs from reading the want ads. Many employers don't advertise at all. They hire people they already know. In fact, most people get jobs using other, "informal" job search methods.

The chart below shows how people actually find jobs. Notice that about two-thirds of all job seekers get their jobs using informal methods.

How People Find Jobs

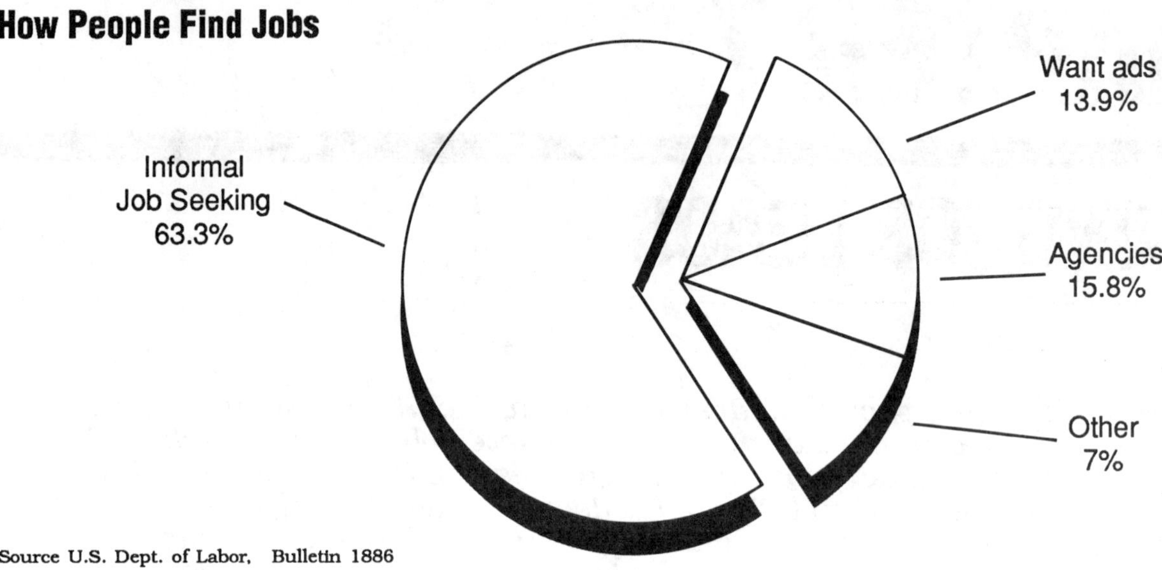

Source U.S. Dept. of Labor, Bulletin 1886

Informal Job Search Methods

There are two basic informal job search methods—"networking" with people you know (warm contacts) and making direct contacts with an employer (cold contacts). They are both based on the most important job search rule of all:

Don't Wait Until The Job Is Open!

Most jobs get filled by someone the employer meets before a job is formally "open." So the trick is to meet people who can hire you *before* a job is available! Instead of saying "Do you have any jobs open?," say "I realize you may not have any openings now, but I would still like to talk to you about the possibility of future openings."

ACTIVITY Networking With Warm Contacts: The Most Effective Job Search Method

Many people find their jobs through a lead provided by a friend, a relative, or an "acquaintance." We call these people "warm contacts" because they know you and are the ones most likely to help. Contacting these people is the most effective job search method for most people. Developing new contacts is called "networking," and here is how it works.

1. **Develop a list of all the groups of people you know.** Begin with your friends and relatives. Then think of other groups of people with whom you have something in common. For example, people you used to work with, people who went to your school, people in social or sports groups you belong to, former employers, members of your religious group.

Groups of People You Know Worksheet

Group	Number	Group	Number
Friends	______	____________________	______
Relatives	______	____________________	______
____________________	______	____________________	______
____________________	______	____________________	______
____________________	______	____________________	______
____________________	______	____________________	______
____________________	______	____________________	______
____________________	______	____________________	______
____________________	______	____________________	______
____________________	______	____________________	______
____________________	______	____________________	______
____________________	______	____________________	______
____________________	______	____________________	______
____________________	______	____________________	______
____________________	______	____________________	______
____________________	______	____________________	______
____________________	______	____________________	______
____________________	______	____________________	______
____________________	______	____________________	______
____________________	______	____________________	______
____________________	______	____________________	______
____________________	______	____________________	______
____________________	______	____________________	______

2. **Develop a separate list for each group of people you know.** Some of the lists, such as your friends or relatives, may be quite large, but don't worry about that. You may not know the names of many of the people from other groups, for example "People who go to my church," but you can get them later. Almost all these people will be willing to help you in your job search!

The worksheet that follows will help you list the people from one of your groups in an organized way. Complete this form for one of the groups you listed, and use additional sheets for other groups. We suggest that you begin by listing your friends or relatives. Don't worry about their phone numbers for now.

Network Contact Worksheet

Group____________________________

Name	Telephone	Name	Telephone

3. **Contact people.** Start with your friends and relatives. Call them and tell them that you are looking for a job and need their help. Be as clear as possible about what you are looking for and about your skills and qualifications. Look at the sample *JIST Card* and phone script elsewhere in this book for presentation ideas.

4. **Ask for leads.** Some of the people you contact may know of a job opening just right for you. If so, get the details and get right on it! More than likely, however, they will not know of an opening, so here are three questions you should ask.

The Three Magic Questions

1. ***"Do you know of any openings for a person with my skills?"***
   If no, then ask:
2. ***"Do you know of someone else who might know of such an opening?"***
   If yes, get that person's name, and ask for another name. If no, then ask:
3. ***"Do you know someone who knows lots of people?"***
   If all else fails, this will usually get you a name.

5. **Keep records.** Keep a record of all your contacts. Simple 3" × 5" index cards are very useful for recording important information, and they are easy to organize. You can get these cards at most stationery stores. Use the following example as a model.

Job Lead Card

Organization: Mutual Health Insurance
Contact Person: Anna Tomey Phone: (317) 355-0216
Source of Lead: Aunt Ruth
Notes: 4/10 Called. Anna on vacation. Call back 4/15
4/15 Interview set 4/20 at 1:30; 4/20 Anna showed me around. They use the same computer we used in school! (Friendly people) Sent thank you note & JIST card. Call back 5/1.
5/1 2nd interview 5/8 at 9 a.m.!

6. **Follow up.** Call the people your contacts suggest and repeat steps 3, 4, and 5. For each original contact, you can extend your network of acquaintances by hundreds of people. It will be like the following illustration. Eventually, one or these people will hire you—or refer you to someone who will!

Tips—Following Up On Network Contacts

- Keep a record of all your contacts.
- Always complete a follow-up card for each one.
- Always have extra index cards on hand.
- Be pleasant and professional in all contacts.
- Each time you contact a person in your "network," send a thank-you note.
- Include a copy of your *JIST Card.*
- Get a card file box (available at stationery stores), and file your job lead cards under the date you want to follow up.

Cold Contacts: Contacting Employers Directly

It takes more courage, but contacting an employer directly is a very effective job search technique. Since most jobs are not advertised, one effective way to find openings is to call employers who might need a person with your skills. The *Yellow Pages* of the phone book is a very good source of places to call. Once you locate an organization that needs your skills, give them a call. Simply ask for the person in charge, and ask to come in for an interview. You will learn more about how to do this later in this chapter.

You can also just walk in and ask to speak to the person in charge. This is particularly effective in small businesses but works surprisingly well in larger ones, too. Remember, you want an interview even if there are no openings now. If your timing is inconvenient, ask for a better time to come back for an interview. It works!

Pay Attention To Small Businesses!

About two out of three of all new jobs are now created by small businesses. While the largest corporations have reduced their number of employees, small businesses have been creating as many as 80 percent of all new jobs. There are many opportunities to obtain training and to advance in smaller organizations, too. Many do not even have a personnel department, so non-traditional job search techniques are particularly effective with them.

Where People Work

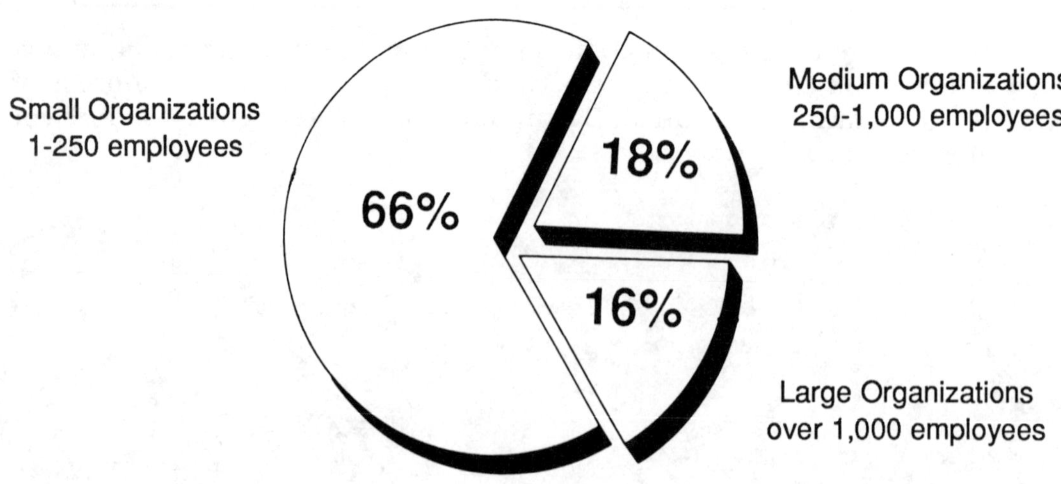

Source: U.S. Dept. of Labor, 1987

ACTIVITY Using The *Yellow Pages*

1. Find the index section in the *Yellow Pages*. This is usually in the front of the book. It lists the various types of businesses and other organizations within each area. (If you do not have a complete copy of the local *Yellow Pages*, there is a sample page from another city's *Yellow Pages* at the end of this chapter. Your instructor will tell you what to do.)
2. For each of these listings ask yourself this question: *"Could this type of organization possibly use a person with my skills?"* (It will help if you have a job objective here, such as "secretary" or "auto mechanic.")
3. Look up the names of at least 10 specific organizations from the *Yellow Pages* listed in the index that might hire people with your skills. Then use the worksheet that follows.

Yellow Pages Worksheet #1 Types of Organizations

From the *Yellow Pages* index, list 10 types of organizations that could use your skills.

1. ______________	6. ______________
2. ______________	7. ______________
3. ______________	8. ______________
4. ______________	9. ______________
5. ______________	10. ______________

Organizing Your *Yellow Pages* Contacts

You can use this same process to go through every listing in the *Yellow Pages* index. This will help you discover many employers that you would normally overlook. For each, ask the same question:

"Could this type of organization possibly use a person with my skills?"

When the answer is "yes," decide how interested you are in working for this type of organization. Write these codes next to each "yes" response in the *Yellow Pages* index:

1 = Very Interested   2 = Somewhat Interested   3 = Not Interested

Go back and put a 1, 2, or 3 by each of the 10 types of organizations you listed in the worksheet above.

Specific Organizations

Next, turn to the *Yellow Pages* section for each type of organization, and list the specific companies or organizations listed there. These organizations are hot prospects for you to contact in your search for a job. Look at the following form to see an example of how this is done. The *Yellow Pages* Worksheet #2 gives you an example of how this information can be organized.

Later, you will learn how to contact each organization and ask for an interview. In this way you can generate many job leads from the "hidden" job market!

Yellow Pages Worksheet #2 Specific Organizations

Yellow Pages Index Listing: ______________________________

Specific Organization	Telephone	Specific Organization	Telephone

Remember

For each contact, follow up with a thank-you note, and include your *JIST Card.*

Traditional Job Search Methods

While the informal methods are more effective for most people, you may want to use some of the more traditional job search methods. Information on the major ones follow.

- **Help Wanted Ads.** As you already know, most jobs are not advertised. But there are problems even with those that are! Everyone who reads the paper knows about those job openings. As a result, the competition for these jobs will be fierce. Still, some people do get jobs this way, so go ahead and apply. Just be sure to spend most of your time using more effective methods.
- **The State Employment Service.** Often called the "Unemployment Office," they do offer free job leads. But they are likely to know of only 10 percent or less of the available jobs in your area. However, it is worth a weekly visit. If you ask for the same counselor, you might impress him or her enough to remember you and refer the better openings to you.
- **Private Employment Agencies.** These are for-profit businesses that charge a fee either to you (as high as 20 percent of your annual salary!) or the employer. They find most job leads by calling employers and asking if they have any openings. This is a technique you will learn to do yourself. Unless you have skills that are in high demand, you will probably do better on your own—and save money, too.
- **Sending Out Resumes.** Sending resumes to people you don't know does not work well for most people. A much better approach is to phone the person who might hire

you in order to set up an interview directly, *then* send a resume. Tips on resume writing and using resumes will be provided in a later chapter of this book.

- **Filling Out Applications.** Most applications are used to screen you out. Larger organizations may require them, but you should remember that your task is to get an interview, not to fill out an application. If you do complete them, make them neat and error free, and do not include anything that could get you screened out. If necessary, leave a problem section blank. You can always explain it after you get an offer.
- **Personnel Departments.** Few people get hired by someone in a Personnel Department. Their job is to screen you out. Be cooperative with them, but try to go directly to the person who is most likely to supervise you, even if there is no opening just now. Remember that most smaller organizations don't even have a personnel office; only the larger ones do!

The Answers For How People Find Jobs

Some job search techniques are more effective than others. Following are figures showing the percentage of people who actually got their jobs by using the various job search techniques. These are the correct answers to the activity at the beginning of this chapter. How close were your answers?

1. 13.9 percent answered help wanted ads, **2.** 28.4 percent heard about an opening from people they knew, **3.** 5.1 percent were referred by a state employment service, **4.** 5.6 percent were referred by a private employment agency, **5.** 34.9 percent contacted employers directly, **6.** 3.0 percent were referred by a school placement office, **7.** 2.1 percent took civil service tests, **8.** 7.0 percent used other miscellaneous methods—union hiring hall, placed ad in journal, etc. (From the U.S. Department of Labor, Bulletin 1886.)

INDEX to the YELLOW PAGES

Real—(Cont'd)
Estate Management 292,293
Estate Rental Service 293
Rebuilt—
Parts-Automotive See
Automobile Parts & Supplies-New 28-30
Automobile Parts & Supplies-Used & Rebuilt 30
Record Players-Coin Operated See
Juke Boxes 197
Recorders—
Sound & Video See
Audio-Visual Equipment-Dealers 25
Video Recorders & Players-Dealers 388
Recording—
Instruments-Industrial & Scientific 293
Service-Sound & Video 293
Studio Equipment-Sound & Video 293
Records—
Phonograph-Mfrs' Equipment & Supplies 293
Phonograph-Whol & Mfrs 293
Stored 293
Recreational—
Vehicles-Equipment, Parts & Supplies 294
Vehicles-Whol & Mfrs 294
Recycling—
Centers 294
Equipment & Systems 294
Equipment & Systems 294
Reducing—
Equipment See
Exercise Equipment 141
Exercise Equipment-Sales & Service 141
Refiners—
See
Oil Refiners 242
Smelters & Refiners-Base Metals 328
Smelters & Refiners-Precious Metals 328
Refractometers—
See
Laboratory Equipment & Supplies 200
Scientific Apparatus & Instruments 314
Testing Apparatus 356
Refractories 294
Refreshment Stands 294
Refrigerating—
Equipment-Commercial-Sales & Service 294,295
Equipment-Supplies & Parts 295
Refrigeration—
Equipment-Truck See
Truck Refrigeration Equipment 372
Supplies & Parts See
Refrigerating Equipment-Supplies & Parts 295
Refrigerators & Freezers Refinishing See
Porcelain Enameling 271
Refrigerators & Freezers-Supplies & Parts 295
Refrigerators & Freezers-Whol & Mfrs 295
Registers—
See
Autographic Registers & Supplies 26
Cash Registers & Supplies 61
Regulators—
See
Controls, Control Systems & Regulators 95-97
Valves 385-387
Rehabilitation Services 295,296
Reinforcements-Concrete See
Concrete Reinforcements 85
Relocation Service 296
Rendering Companies 296
Rental—
Agencies-Housing See
Real Estate Rental Service 293
Buses See
Buses-Charter & Rental 53
Service Stores & Yards 296
Replacement Windows See
Windows 401
Reporters-Court & Convention 296,297
Repossessing Service 297
Research—
Laboratories See
Chemists-Analytical & Consulting 65
Laboratories-Research & Development 199
Services See
Economic Research & Analysis 122
Educational Research 122
Electronics Research & Development 130
Information Search & Retrieval Service 179
Laboratories-Research & Development 199
Library Research Service 205
Market Research & Analysis 223
Plastics-Research & Consulting 265
Solar Energy Research, Development & Design 329
Resins 297
Resistors 297
Resorts 297
Rest Room Deodorizing & Disinfecting See
Deodorizing & Disinfecting 114
Restaurant—
Equipment Repairing & Servicing 297
Equipment & Supplies 298,299
Facilities Consultants See
Food Facilities Consultants 155
Management 299
Retirement Insurance See
Insurance 180-191
Retirement Planning Services 299
Revolving Doors See
Doors 117
Rheostats—
See
Controls, Control Systems & Regulators 95-97
Welding Equipment & Supplies 398-400
Ribbons 299
Rice 299
Riding—
Mowers See
Lawn Mowers-Whol & Mfrs 203
Rifles—
See
Guns & Gunsmiths 165
Riggers 299
Rims-Wheels See
Wheels 400
Riveting Equipment 300
Rivets 300
Roach Exterminating See
Pest Control Services 259,260
Road—
Building Contractors 300
Building Equipment 300
Oiling & Dust Control 300
Robes, Caps & Gowns 300
Robot Systems See
Automation Systems & Equipment 26,27
Robots & Robotic Systems 300
Rock—
Salt See
Salt 309
Rods-Threaded 300
Roller—
Bearings See
Bearings 38
Rollers-Wooden, Metal, Rubber, Etc. 300
Rolling—
Doors See
Doors 117
Roof—
Decks 300
Structures 300
Trusses See
Roof Structures 300
Trusses-Construction 381
Roofing—
Contractors 300-305
Equipment & Supplies 305
Materials 305
Service Consultants 305
Room—
Additions See
Building Contractors 46-48
Carpenters 58
Contractors-Alteration 86
Rope 305
Rope—
Wire See
Wire Rope 402
Rotary Joints 305
Routing Service-Air, Highway & Marine 305
Rubbage Compactors See
Waste Reduction, Disposal & Recycling Equipment-Industrial 393
Rubber—
Belting See
Belting & Belting Supplies 39
Cement See
Adhesives & Glues 6
Coatings See
Coatings-Protective 68
Foam & Sponge See
Foam & Sponge Rubber 155
Hose & Tubing See
Hose & Tubing-Rubber & Plastic 172
Mats See
Mats & Matting 226
Molds See
Molds 232,233
Rubber & Plastic Stamps See
Rubber Stamps 306
Rubber—
Printing Plates See
Printing Plates 276
Products 306
Stamps 306
Stamps-Mfrs Equipment & Supplies 306
Type Marking Stamps See
Marking & Coding Equipment 223
Rubbing Compounds See
Abrasives 1
Rubbish—
Compactors See
Compactors-Waste-Industrial & Commercial 70
Rubbish & Garbage Removal Contractors Equipment 308
Rubbish & Garbage Removal 306-308
Rubbish & Garbage Removal Contractors Equipment 308
Rug—
Cleaners' Supplies See
Carpet & Rug Cleaning Equipment & Supplies 59
Dyers See
Carpet & Rug Dyers 61
Rust Preventives & Removers 308
Rustproofing-Industrial 308
Rustproofing & Undercoating-Automotive 308

S

Sacks-Paper See
Bags-Paper 33
Safes & Vaults 308
Safes & Vaults-Opening & Repairing 308
Safety—
Belts See
Safety Equipment & Clothing 308,309
Cans 308
Consultants 308
Equipment & Clothing 308,309
Salads 309
Sales—
Incentive Programs See
Incentive Programs 178
Sales Promotion Service 309
Sales—
Organizations 309
Presentations 309
Promotion Service 309
Training 309
Salt 309
Salvage—
Computer Equipment See
Computers-Dealers-Used 77
Salvage & Surplus Merchandise See
Surplus & Salvage Merchandise 342
Sample—
Cases 309
Sample & Circular Distributing See
Advertising-Direct Mail 8,9
Sample & Circular Distributing See
Distributing Service-Circular, Sample, Etc. 116
Sample & Circular Distributing See
Sales Promotion Service 309
Sand Bags See
Barricades 37
Sand & Gravel 309,310
Sandblasting 310
Sandblasting Equipment & Supplies 310
Sanding—
Floor See
Floor Laying, Refinishing & Resurfacing 153
Machines See
Floor Machines 153,154
Tools-Electric 362,363
Woodworking Equipment & Supplies 403
Machines-Renting See
Rental Service Stores & Yards 296
Sandwiches—
Whol 310
Sanitary Napkins 310
Satellite—
Equipment & Systems 310,311
Sauna—
Equipment & Supplies 311
Savings—
Accounts See
Banks 34-37
Savings & Loan Associations 311
Savings & Loan Associations 311
Sawmills 311
Saws 311
Saws-Sharpening & Repairing 311
Scaffolding & Aerial Lifts 312
Scales 313,314
Scales—
Public 314
Repairing 314
Scenery Studios 314
School Buses See
Buses-Distrs & Mfrs 53
School—
Furniture & Equipment 314
Supplies 314
Schools—
See
Computers-Instruction 77
First Aid Instruction 152
Language Schools 202
Scientific Apparatus & Instruments 314
Scissors-Sharpening See
Sharpening Service 321
Scrap—
Film 314
Metals 314,315
Screen—
Mfrs Equipment & Supplies 315
Printing 315,316
Printing-Equipment & Supplies 316
Screening & Sifting Equipment 316
Screens—
Door & Window 316
Screw—
Machine Products 316,317
Screws 317
Scuba Divers' Equipment & Supplies See
Divers' Equipment & Supplies 116
Seafood—
See
Fish & Seafood-Whol 152
Seal Coating See
Asphalt & Asphalt Products 24
Sealants—
See
Adhesives & Glueing Equipment 6
Adhesives & Glues 6
Sealers—
Asphalt & Concrete See
Coatings-Protective 68
Concrete Curing & Treating Materials 84
Paving Materials 257
Waterproofing Materials 397
Sealing—
Compounds See
Caulking Materials & Equipment 63
Roofing Materials 305
Machines See
Tape Applying & Dispensing Machines 345
Seals—
Mechanical 317
Notary & Corporation 317
O-Ring 317
Oil, Grease, Etc. 317
Seamless—
Floors See
Floor Materials-Whol & Mfrs 154
Seating Companies 317
Secretarial—
Services 317
Securities—
Investment See
Investment Securities 193,194
Mutual Funds 237
Stock & Bond Brokers 339
Security—
Control Consultants 317
Control Equipment & Systems 318
Dog Service See
Guard Dogs 165
Guard & Patrol Service 318
Seeds & Bulbs-Whol 318
Semiconductor Devices 318
Septic—
Tanks & Systems-Cleaning 318,319
Tanks & Systems-Contractors & Dealers 319
Tanks & Systems-Whol & Mfrs 319
Serums 319
Service—
Station Equipment & Supplies 319,320
Sewage—
Disposal Systems 320
Plant Operation 320
Treatment Chemicals See
Chemicals-Dlrs 65
Chemicals-Whol & Mfrs 65
Treatment Equipment 320
Sewer—
Cleaning Equipment & Supplies 320
Contractors 320,321
Pipe 321
Pipe & Tile See
Building Materials-Whol & Mfrs 49
System Inspection Service 321
Sewing—
Contractors 321
Machines-Industrial & Commercial 321
Shades—
Window See
Window Shades 401
Sharpening—
Service 321
Shear Knives See
Knives-Machine 197
Shearing—
Metal See
Metal Slitting & Shearing 228
Steel Processing 339
Sheet—
Metal Fabricators 321
Metal Work 321,322
Metal Working Equipment & Supplies 322
Shelving 322-324
Shingles 324
Shipping—
Containers See
Boxes-Corrugated & Fiber 44,45
Boxes-Wire Bound 45
Boxes-Wooden 45
Room Supplies 324
Shirt Lettering Service See
Monograms 233
Shirts—
Custom Made 324
Whol & Mfrs 324
Shoes—
Whol & Mfrs 324
Shop Equipment 324
Shopping—
Carts & Baskets 324
Shoring—
Equipment 324
Shot—
Blasting See
Sandblasting 310
Peening 324
Shotguns—
See
Guns & Gunsmiths 165
Show—
Cards See
Signs 325-328
Cases 324
Shower—
Doors & Enclosures 324
Shredders—
See
Paper Shredding Machines 253,254
Waste Reduction, Disposal & Recycling Equipment-Industrial 393
Shrubbery—
See
Nurseries-Plants, Trees, Etc. 238
Sickroom—
Supplies See
Hospital Equipment & Supplies 172,173
Sidewalk Contractors See
Concrete Contractors 83,84
Siding—
Cleaning See
Building Cleaning-Exterior 46
Contractors 324,325
Materials 325
Sifting Equipment See
Screening & Sifting Equipment 316
Sightseeing Tours 325
Sign Letters See
Letters-Sign 204
Signaling & Paging Equipment See
Paging & Signaling Equipment & Systems 248,249
Signs 325-328
Signs—
Equipment & Supplies 328
Erectors & Hangers 328
Maintenance & Repairing 328
Silencers-Industrial 328
Silicones 328
Silk Screen Processing Equipment & Supplies See
Screen Printing-Equipment & Supplies 316
Silks-Wholesale & Mfrs 328
Silos 328
Silver—
Plating See
Plating 266,267
Silversmiths & Goldsmiths 328
Silversmiths & Goldsmiths 328
Sinks—
Repairing & Refinishing See
Bathtubs & Sinks-Repairing & Refinishing 38
Ski—
Trips & Tours See
Tours-Operators & Promoters 364
Travel Agencies & Bureaus 368,369
Skid Steer Loaders See
Contractors' Equipment & Supplies-Dealers & Service 86-88
Skids & Pallets See
Pallets & Skids 251,252
Skin—
Diving Equipment & Supplies See
Divers' Equipment & Supplies 116
Sporting Goods-Whol & Mfrs 331
Skip Tracing 328
Sky—
Writing See
Advertising-Aerial 6
Skylights 328
Slate 328
Slaughter—
Houses See
Butchering 55
Meat-Whol 226
Sleeping—
Bags See
Sporting Goods-Whol & Mfrs 331
Slicing Machines 328
Slides & Film Strips 328
Sliding Doors See
Doors 117
Slings 328
Slitting—
Metal See
Metal Slitting & Shearing 228
Steel Processing 339
Slush Drinks See
Beverage Distributors & Bottlers 39
Smelters & Refiners-Base Metals 328
Smelters & Refiners-Precious Metals 328
Smoke—
Detectors & Alarms 328
Odor Counteracting Service 329
Stacks 329
Snow—
Blower Engines See
Engines-Gasoline 138
Removal Service 329
Soaps & Detergents 329
Sod & Sodding Service 329
Soda—
Fountain Equipment 329
Soft—
Drink Vending Machines See
Vending Machines 387
Water Service See
Water Softening & Conditioning Equipment, Service & Supplies 395,396
Softeners Water See
Water Softening & Conditioning Equipment, Service & Supplies 395,396
Soil—
See
Topsoil 364
Analysis See
Chemists-Analytical & Consulting 65
Laboratories-Testing 199,200
Conservation Service 329

CONTINUED FROM PAGE 52

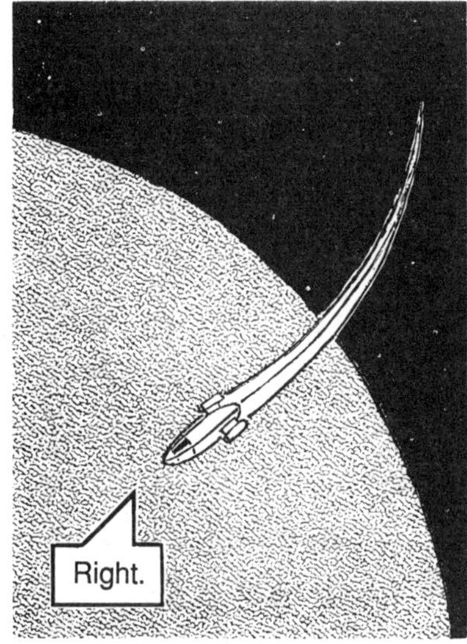

MEANWHILE: At a space base on the planet below, Commander Jack "Astro" Turph ponders a ponderous dilemma.

For this JIST SO STORY, I've set the ol' Chronobrator for the year 1876. Our destination is the laboratory of that renowned scientist, Alexander Graham Bell. We're going to witness a major historical event—THE FIRST TELEPHONE CONTACT!

CONTINUED ON PAGE 71

CHAPTER 8

DIALING FOR DOLLARS: USING THE TELEPHONE

Remember that most jobs are never advertised. They are found in the "hidden" job market. One way to find this market is by telephone.

Your task in this chapter is to discover the many ways the telephone can help uncover these hidden jobs.

Why The Telephone?

Using the telephone in your job search offers many advantages:

- **Time and Money.** Most people can learn to call 10 to 20 employers in one hour. You might spend a whole day contacting this many employers in person.
- **New Opportunities.** By calling a potential employer directly, you can often uncover leads for jobs long before they will be advertised. They may even create a job for you because you sound like the right person with the right skills for their organization.
- **A Positive Impression.** Good telephone use can create a positive impression. This will give you the edge over those who simply fill out an application or send in a resume.
- **Getting Directly to the Hiring Authority.** Using the phone makes it much easier to get directly to the person who is likely to supervise someone with your skills. It is much more effective than filling out applications or sending in resumes.
- **Results.** People who use the telephone well can get many more interviews than people using traditional methods. Many will also get job offers sooner.

You Can Do It!

Many people find it hard to make phone calls to employers they don't know. They are afraid of being rejected. But preparation can make it much easier. The two most important things to do are:

1. Know what you are going to say in advance.
2. Practice your telephone presentation by yourself and with others until you feel prepared to make calls to employers.

A Sample Telephone Script

Your *JIST Card*, with just a few changes, can form the basis for an effective telephone script. Here is an example based on a *JIST Card* presented in Chapter 6:

May I speak to the person in charge of auto repair?

Hello, my name is John Kijek. I am interested in a position as an auto mechanic. I have over three years of work experience including one year in a full-time auto training program. I am familiar with all hand tools and basic diagnostic equipment and can handle most common repairs including tune-ups, brakes, exhaust systems, electrical and mechanical work. I am also a fast worker, often completing jobs in less than standard time. I have a complete set of tools and can start work immediately on any shift.

I am honest, reliable, and good with people.

When may I come in for an interview?

How Does It Sound To You?

If you were an employer and hired people with similar skills, how would you feel about someone saying this to you on the phone? Would you give him an interview?

____

____

____

When asked this same question, most employers say they would interview this person. They were interested enough in what the person said to consider him for a future opening—even if they did not have one right away! From beginning to end, this phone script takes less than 30 seconds to say out loud. And yet many employers have granted interviews on just this much information. The telephone script based on your *JIST Card* is a powerful tool. In the next activity, you will learn how to create your own script.

ACTIVITY Preparing Your Telephone Script

The 6 Parts to a JIST Phone Script

There are six basic parts to a phone contact. They are:

1. **The Target**—the person who would supervise you.
2. **The Name**—who you are.
3. **The Job**—what you want to do.
4. **The Hook**—what you have to offer.
5. **The Goal**—to get an interview or a referral.
6. **The Closing**—saying thank you and goodbye.

Each of these parts is covered in the worksheet below. Use the information from your own *JIST Card* to fill out each section. Because we speak differently than we write, change the content of your *JIST Card* so that it "sounds natural" as you speak it.

Before you complete the worksheet itself, use separate sheets of paper to create a rough draft of each worksheet section. Edit your material until you feel that it sounds good enough to write on the worksheet. Then complete each section of the worksheet with your final draft.

Telephone Contact Worksheet

The Target: *May I please speak to the person in charge of:* ______________________________

____

The Name: *Hello, my name is:* ______________________________

The Job: *I am interested in a position as:* ______________________________

____

The Hook: *Include details from the "skills" section of your* ***JIST Card*** *here.*

____

____

____

____

____

____

____

____

____

The Goal: *When may I come in for an interview?* If you are unable to get an interview, ask, *Do you know of any other organizations that would need someone with my skills?*

____

____

____

____

____

____

The Closing: *Thank you very much for your time. I'll see you on:*________________ (date and time) *for my interview.*

Practice!

Keep rewriting your telephone script until it sounds "right." The first five parts of the final version should take you between 25 and 30 seconds to read aloud in a conversational style. Remember to say it slowly and distinctly so that you can be understood. Then practice saying it aloud by yourself and to others. You will quickly feel more comfortable with your presentation and be able to say it more smoothly.

ACTIVITY Advanced Telephone Techniques

You now have a script to use in your phone calls. When you actually make your phone calls, you need to be prepared to handle several common problems. Here are some examples:

- How do you get past the secretary or receptionist who is trained to screen calls such as the one you are making?
- How do you respond to "Sorry, there are no openings"?
- How do you avoid an interview over the phone?

These are just a few of the situations that you may encounter as you make your telephone contacts. To overcome them, you need to have clear objectives as well as a few techniques to help you meet them. Here are some guidelines to help you develop effective telephone skills.

Telephone Contact Goals

- **Get through to the hiring authority,** the one person most likely to supervise you.
- **Present your entire script.** Do this clearly and without interruption.
- **Get an interview!** Be prepared to ask all *three* questions:
  1. For the position you want. If *no*, then...
  2. To discuss future openings. If *no*, then...
  3. For information about the organization.
- **If you do not get an interview:**
  1. Get a referral.
  2. Set up a date and time to call back.

Learning To Overcome Typical Problems

Here are some common situations that you may experience when making calls. Notice how they are handled, and compare their approach to those suggested in the previous section. Do the sample responses meet the goals of a good telephone contact?

Situation 1

You ask to speak to the manager, supervisor, or director in charge of the job you are seeking. You ***do not*** *want to get referred to a Personnel Department, told there are no openings, or screened out by the receptionist. The receptionist wants to know why you are calling.*

Prepare a response using the following tips:

- Sound businesslike and friendly. Act as if you *expect* you will get to the person you want to speak with. Begin by asking for the name of the person in charge of the area where you want to work. Then ask to be connected. In most cases, this will get you through.
- If you have been referred to the person you are calling, say that someone—a friend of the person you are calling—suggested you call.
- If you feel that you are being screened out, say that you want to send some material to the person and you need the correct spelling of the name, title, and address. (This is true, since you will be sending a resume and *JIST Card* later.) Then call back tomorrow and ask for the person by name or call during lunch, when a replacement receptionist is on the phone.

Situation 2

The supervisor tells you there are no openings at the present time.

Prepare a response using the following tips:

- Don't give up! Show that you are still interested, and again ask for an interview. They will often consider a second request.
- Say that although there are no openings at present, you are still very interested and would like to come in anyway to discuss any future openings.
- If you can't get an interview, *then*:
- Ask if it is OK to stay in touch and, if so, if you can call back in about two weeks. You might also ask for the name of any other organization that might need someone with your skills.

Situation 3

Because of your good presentation, the employer shows an interest in you and begins to ask you questions over the phone.

Prepare a response using the following tips:

- Ask if you can schedule an interview to allow you to cover in person any questions he or she might have. If that doesn't work *then*:
- Tell him or her more about your special skills, experience, or training that qualify you for the job.
- Explain why you would be a good employee for this company.
- Ask questions about the company's service or products. (Do *not* ask about pay or benefits!)
- Close with a request for an interview.

Remember: **Your Main Goal Is To Get An Interview!**

Assignment

Write out a final phone script based on your *JIST Card.* Write it just as you will say it out loud on the phone. Turn it in for grading at the next session.

Practice your phone contact replies by yourself and with others until you feel comfortable with them and can say them smoothly. Get ready to begin your real telephone contacts.

CONTINUED FROM PAGE 64

Hear, right here, Dear, the Top 40 smash hit of the year from "THE QUADRAPHONIX"—that popular choral group featuring the Hider Brothers, a set of Siamese quadruplets connected at the shoulders and the paycheck.

CHAPTER 9

THE INTERVIEW

Very few people get a job without an interview. It is a very important part of the job search process. The interview provides employers the chance to get to know you. It provides you with the same opportunity—a chance to get to know them.

The Interview And Employer's Expectations

The interview is the time to show that you can meet the three employer expectations: *Appearance, Dependability, Skills!*

Appearance

There are several appearance-related details an employer will evaluate when interviewing an individual for a job. They are:

- **Personal appearance.** If your appearance is "wrong," it will turn off an employer immediately. Different jobs require different dress and grooming fc r the interview. A simple rule is:

  > *Dress as the interviewer is likely to dress—**only cleaner!***

- **Manner.** Arrive early and be relaxed. Greet the employer in a friendly way, and shake hands if it is offered. During the interview, be aware of how you look to the interviewer. For example, leaning forward a bit in your chair helps you look interested and alert. Smiling and looking at the interviewer as he or she speaks helps you seem more confident.
- **Paperwork.** Your application, *JIST Card,* and resume create an impression, too. Are they neat, error free, accurate, and filled out completely?
- **Communications.** Speak in a distinct and clear voice. Use proper grammar. Emphasize the things you can do well and a willingness to try hard. Be honest and open with your answers.

Dependability

Above all else, employers want to hire people they can trust to do the job. They need people they can count on. Many of the questions an employer asks during the interview will give you a chance to show that you are dependable. It is *very* important that you tell them!

Skills

The employer will want to know what you can do. Review your skills lists from Chapter 3 to help remind yourself of what you can do. Since you will probably compete with job seekers who have more work experience than you, emphasize your self-management and transferable skills in your interview responses.

A Technique For Answering Interview Questions

There are hundreds of questions an interviewer might ask you in an interview. It would be impossible for you to have answers prepared for all of them. A better approach is to learn a *technique* to answering most interview questions.

Three Steps To Answering Problem Questions

1. ***Understand what is really being asked.***
   Most questions are really trying to find out about your self- management skills. While employers are rarely this blunt, the employer's *real* questions are often:
   - Can I depend on you?
   - Are you easy to get along with?
   - Are you a good worker?

   The question may also be:
   - Do you have the experience and training to do the job il I hire you?
2. ***Answer the question briefly.***
   - Acknowledge the facts, but...
   - Present them as an advantage, not a disadvantage.
3. ***Answer the real concern by presenting your related skills.***
   - Base your answer on your key skills from your lists in Chapter 3.
   - Give examples to support your skills statements.

A Sample Response

For example, let's say the question is:

"We were looking for someone with more experience in this field. Why should we consider you?"

Here is one possible answer:

"I'm sure there are people who have more experience. But I do have over three years of work experience including one year of advanced training and hands-on experience using the latest methods and techniques. Because my training is recent, I am open to new ideas and am used to working hard and learning quickly."

Whatever your situation, learn to use it to your advantage! Use the three-step process to answer interview questions. It works!

ACTIVITY Answering Problem Questions

This activity includes interview questions that many job seekers do not answer well. They are also the ones most likely to be asked during an interview. If you can give good answers to them, you will be able to handle most other interview questions, too.

Problem Questions Worksheet

Review your top transferable, self-management, and job-related skills along with the examples you used to back them up.

Write a rough draft from all your notes and ideas before you write your answers on the worksheet provided below. Write complete responses for each question using the *Three-Step Process for Answering Interview Questions*. Use additional paper if needed.

Can you tell me a little about yourself?____________________

Why are you applying for this type of job and why here?____________________

What kind of training or experience do you have in this field?____________________

Problem Questions Worksheet

What are the greatest strengths you would bring to this job?

What do you consider your greatest weakness?

How much do you expect to be paid?

Can you tell me about a problem you had on your previous job and how you handled it?

How can you help us make more money or do better as an organization?

Problem Questions Worksheet

What would you consider to be an *ideal* job for you? ______________________________

Can you tell me why you consider yourself a responsible person? ______________________________

What are your interests and things you like to do most? ______________________________

Why should I offer you the job? ______________________________

Questions You Might Ask An Employer

Most interviewers will invite you to ask questions about the job or organization. The following are tips on things you can ask — and a few things to avoid.

Questions To Ask

Ask questions that show you are interested in doing a good job and are interested in getting ahead. Some examples include:

- What types of training or schooling are available?
- What tools and equipment will you use?
- What can you do to get ahead?
- What is particularly important to do well in this job?

Questions To Avoid

Employers are interested in what you can do for them, not what you want from the employer. For this reason it is often wise to avoid questions about pay, vacations, fringe benefits, and similar issues until the job is offered.

List other questions you can ask to demonstrate your interest in doing well.

Closing The Interview

Most people are not offered the job at the close of the first interview. However, there are things you can do in order to make a good impression before you leave.

The Call-Back Close

- Thank the interviewer by name.
- Express interest in the job and organization.
- Say that you have other interviews and would like to set a day and time to check back.
- Ask for the job. If you want it, say so.
- Thank the interviewer for his or her time, and say good-bye.

Put these tips and any others you feel are best for you in the appropriate section of the *Data Minder.*

After The Interview: Follow Up!

Be sure to send a thank-you letter or note after your interview. It is best to send this the same day if at all possible. A sample thank-you letter is provided in Chapter 10 to give you some ideas. Also complete or update a Job Lead Card as described in Chapter 7. Remind yourself to call the interviewer back by filing the Job Lead Card under a specific date in your file box.

make your rez´ōō-mā´ pay!

Lesson One: You have to have a resume before you can begin to make one pay. Right? Right! Write! Read this chapter and write your own superior resume.

Lesson Two: After you make your resume, put it to superior use. Get it to the people who can help, recommend, or hire you.

Don't mail out hundreds of resumes at random. Contrary to popular belief, a mass-mailing campaign is a waste of time, money, and good resumes.

On average, out of every 245 resumes sent randomly to employers, only 1 will get you an interview.

And who knows what becomes of the other 244 unsolicited resumes?!

Your resume will be neat and well-written. It will be a confident declaration of the special skills, abilities, and experience that you have to offer. So don't allow your resume to suffer this sort of humiliation.

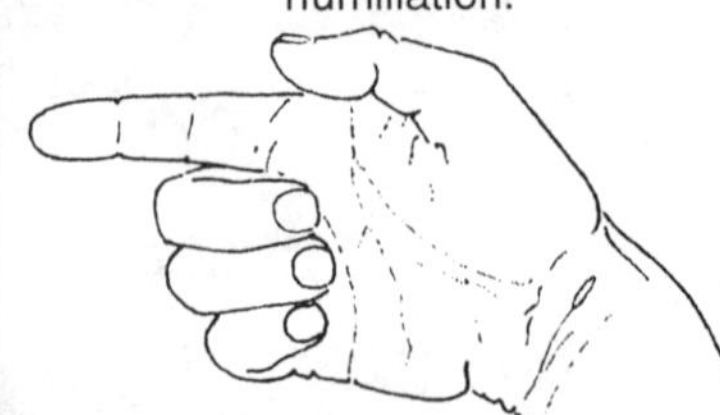

Target any and every person who can help, recommend, or hire you. **And make *your* resume pay!**

CHAPTER 10

SUPERIOR RESUMES, COVER LETTERS, AND THANK-YOU NOTES

You have already learned that sending out resumes is not an effective job-seeking technique, but many employers will ask you for them because they are a useful tool in sorting out potential employees from unsuited individuals.

A well-done resume will tell an employer who you are and how to contact you. It will give a brief review of your background, work, education, life experience, skills, and abilities in a more detailed manner than the information found on your ***JIST Card.***

Types Of Resumes

There are two general types of resumes: chronological and skills. A third type, called a "combination" resume, uses elements of the others. All will be covered in this chapter.

The Chronological Resume

This is the resume format most people use. It is a simple resume that presents experience in reverse chronological order; the most recent experience is listed first, followed by previous experience. If you do not have much work experience, a chronological resume may not be the best one for you to use.

Sample Chronological Resumes: Judith Jones

Look at the following resumes of Judith Jones. Both are chronological resumes, but notice that the second resume includes improvements over the "simple" resume.

The "Simple" Chronological Resume Example

Judith J. Jones
115 South Hawthorne Avenue
Chicago, Illinois 46204

(317) 653-9217 (home)
(317) 272-7608 (message)

JOB OBJECTIVE

Desire a position in the office management, secretarial or clerical area. Prefer a position requiring responsibility and a variety of tasks.

EDUCATION AND TRAINING

Acme Business College, Indianapolis, Indiana — Graduate of a one-year business/secretarial program, 1989.

John Adams High School, South Bend, Indiana — Diploma, business education.

U.S. Army — Financial procedures, accounting functions.

Other: Continuing education classes and workshops in business communication, scheduling systems, and customer relations.

EXPERIENCE

1986-1989 — Returned to school to complete and update my business skills. Learned word processing and other new office techniques.

1985-1986 — Claims Processor, Blue Spear Insurance Co., Indianapolis, Indiana. Handled customer medical claims, used a CRT, filed, miscellaneous clerical duties.

1984-1985 — Sales Clerk, Judy's Boutique, Indianapolis, Indiana. Responsible for counter sales, display design, and selected tasks.

1982-1984 — E4, U.S. Army. Assigned to various stations as a specialist in finance operations. Promoted prior to honorable discharge.

Previous jobs — Held part-time and summer jobs throughout high school.

PERSONAL

I am reliable, hard working, and good with people.

The "Improved" Chronological Resume Example

The "improved" resume is clearly a better resume, but both would be acceptable to most employers.

Judith J. Jones
115 South Hawthorne Avenue
Chicago, Illinois 46204

(317) 653-9217 (home)
(317) 272-7608 (message)

POSITION DESIRED

Seeking position requiring excellent management and secretarial skills in office environment. Position could require a variety of tasks including typing, word processing, accounting/bookkeeping functions, and customer contact.

EDUCATION AND TRAINING

Acme Business College, Indianapolis, Indiana. Completed one-year program in Professional Secretarial and Office Management. Grades in top 30 percent of my class. Courses: word processing, accounting theory and systems, time management, basic supervision and others.

John Adams High School, South Bend, Indiana. Graduated with emphasis on business and secretarial courses. Won shorthand contest.

Other: Continuing education at my own expense (Business Communications, Customer Relations, Computer Applications, other courses).

EXPERIENCE

1986-1989 — Returned to Business School to update skills. Advanced coursework in accounting and office management. Learned to operate word processing equipment including Wang, IBM, DEC. Gained operating knowledge of computers.

1985-1986 — Claims Processor, Blue Spear Insurance Company, Indianapolis, Indiana. Handled 50 complex medical insurance claims per day — 18 percent above department average. Received two merit raises for performance.

1984-1985 — Assistant Manager, Judy's Boutique, Indianapolis, Indiana. Managed sales, financial records, inventory, purchasing, correspondence, and related tasks during owner's absence. Supervised four employees. Sales increased 15 percent during my tenure.

1982-1984 — Finance Specialist (E4), U.S. Army. Responsible for the systematic processing of 500 invoices per day from commercial vendors. Trained and supervised eight employees. Devised internal system allowing 15 percent increase in invoices processed with a decrease in personnel.

1978-1982 — Various part-time and summer jobs through high school. Learned to deal with customers, meet deadlines, and other skills.

SPECIAL SKILLS AND ABILITIES

Type 80 words per minute on electric typewriter, more on word processor; can operate most office equipment. Good math skills. Accept supervision, able to supervise others. Excellent attendance record.

PERSONAL

I have excellent references, learn quickly, and am willing to relocate.

ACTIVITY Chronological Resume Worksheet

Use the worksheet that follows to organize your personal information. Review Chapters 3 through 6 for the skills and other details to use in your worksheet. Later, you can use the information from this worksheet to easily create your chronological resume.

Chronological Resume Worksheet

IDENTIFICATION

- **Name.** Use your formal name rather than a nickname if it sounds more professional.
- **Address.** Be complete. Include zip code and avoid abbreviations. If you may move, use the address of a friend or relative, or be certain to include a forwarding address.
- **Telephone number.** If your home number is often left unanswered during the day, include an alternate number where a message can be left. A reliable friend or relative will usually agree to this, but you could also get an answering machine. Employers are most likely to try to reach you by phone, so having a reliable way to be reached is *very* important.

Name:______________________________

Street Address:______________________________

City/State/Zip:______________________________

Home Phone:______________________________

Alternate Phone: ______________________________

JOB OBJECTIVE

- **Job objective.** The job objective is optional for a very basic resume but important to include whenever possible.
- **Type of position.** Your job objective should include the type of position you want and the skills you want to use.
- **Keep your options open.** Look at Judy's as an example. Saying "Secretary" or "Clerical" might limit her to lower paying jobs or *keep* her from being considered for jobs she might take. Or, instead of "Restaurant Manager," say "Managing a small to mid-sized business," if that is what you are qualified to do.

____

____

____

____

____

____

Chronological Resume Worksheet

EDUCATION AND TRAINING

- **Job-related training.** This is experience! Include details of what you can do.
- **Informal training.** Include informal training here if it relates to the job.
- **Extracurricular activities.** Mention extracurricular activities that indicate you are a hard worker or that show other skills.
- **Accomplishments.** Think about any special accomplishments while in school and include these if they relate to the job. Did you work full time while in school? Do particularly well in work-related classes? Get an award? Participate in sports?

High School: ____________________

City and State: ____________________

Achievements, related activities and courses: ____________________

Vocational High School: ____________________

City and State: ____________________

Achievements, related activities and courses: ____________________

Additional Training or Certification: ____________________

EXPERIENCE

- **If you don't have "experience."** Employers don't expect new grads to have much paid work experience. Include what you *do* have, then include volunteer, family, and other unpaid responsibilities here. They can be handled the same as any other job.
- **Emphasize skills.** Think of the self-management and transferable skills needed in the job you want. Then think of the times you demonstrated these in previous jobs or other activities. Include the best examples in your resume.
- **Use numbers.** If you served 250 people a day for 10 months at the hamburger place, and each customer spent about $4.00, say "Direct customer contacts with over 50,000 people. Handled total sales volume of over $200,000." It's impressive!
- **Job titles and promotions.** Mention any raises or promotions you got. If you did more than your job title indicates, change the title to one that is more descriptive. Use "Head Waiter and Assistant Manager" if that is what you did, rather than "Waiter."

Most Recent or Present Job Title: ____________________

Dates: From ____________________ To ____________________

Organization Name: ____________________

Organization Address: ____________________

Duties and Responsibilities: ____________________

____

____

____

Chronological Resume Worksheet

PERSONAL INFORMATION, HOBBIES, REFERENCES, ETC.

- **Personal data.** Neither of the sample resumes has the standard height, weight, health, or marital status included on so many resumes. That information is simply not necessary! If you do include some personal information, put it at the bottom and keep it related to the job you want.
- **Hobbies.** Unless your hobbies support your job objective or indicate that you are hard working or have other skills, don't include them.
- **References.** There is no need to list references. Nor is it necessary to say "References available upon request." If employers want them, they will ask. If your references are particularly good, it is okay to say so.

The Skills And Combination Resumes

Besides the chronological format, the functional or "skills" resume is often used. This resume lists your most important *skills*, supported by specific examples of how you have used them.

This approach allows you to use any part of your paid or nonpaid experiences to support your ability to do the job you want. If you don't have much work experience, this may be the resume to use.

Tips—Effective Resumes

- Look at the sample resumes for ideas.
- Emphasize skills that are important in the job you want.
- Some skills resumes also include a separate work experience section. These are called "combination" resumes.

Basic Skills Resume Example

ALAN ATWOOD
3231 East Harbor Road
Grand Rapids, MI 41103

Home: **(303) 447-2111**
Message: **(303) 547-8201**

Objective: A responsible position in retail sales

Areas of Accomplishment

Customer Service

- Communicate well with all age groups.
- Able to interpret customer concerns to help them find the items they want.
- Received six Employee of the Month awards in three years.

Merchandise Display

- Developed display skills via in-house training and experience.
- Received Outstanding Trainee Award for Christmas Toy Display.
- Dressed mannequins, arranged table displays, and organized sale merchandise.

Stock Control and Marketing

- Maintained and marked stock during department manager's six-week illness.
- Developed more efficient record-keeping procedures.

Additional Skills

- Operate cash register, IBM compatible hardware, calculators, and electronic typewriters.
- Punctual, honest, reliable, and a hard-working self-starter.

Experience

- Harper's Department Store, Grand Rapids, MI 1987 to Present

Education

- Central High School, Grand Rapids, MI 3.6/4.0 grade point average
- Honor graduate in Distributive Education
- Two years retail sales training in Distributive Education. Also courses in business writing, accounting, typing, and word processing.

Advanced Skills Resume Example

LILI LI LU

1536 Sierra Way • Piedmont, California 97435 • Telephone 436-3874

OBJECTIVE

Program Development, Coordination and Administration

Especially in a people-oriented organization where there is a need to assure broad cooperation through the use of sound planning and strong administration and persuasive skills to achieve community goals.

MAJOR AREAS OF EXPERTISE AND ABILITY

Budgeting and Management for Sound Program Development

With partner, established new association devoted to maximum personal development and self-realization for each of its members. Over a period of time, administered budget totaling $285,000. Jointly planned growth of group and related expenditures, investments, programs, and development of property holdings to realize current and long-term goals. As a result, holdings increased 25 fold over the period, reserves invested increased 1200%, and all major goals for members have been achieved.

Purchasing to Assure Smooth Flow of Needed Supplies and Services

Made most purchasing decisions to ensure maximum production from available funds. Maintained continuous stock inventory to meet on-going needs, selected suppliers, ensured proper disbursements to achieve a strong continuing line of credit while minimizing financing costs.

Transportation Management

Determined transportation needs of group. Assured maximum utilization of limited motor pool. Arranged four major moves of all facilities, furnishings, and equipment to new locations — two across country.

Other Functions Performed

Crisis management, proposal preparation, political analysis, nutrition, recreation planning and administration, stock market operations, taxes, community organization, social affairs administration (including VIP entertaining), landscaping (two awards for excellence), contract negotiations, teaching, and more.

SOME SPECIFIC RESULTS

Above experience gained in 20 years devoted to family development and household management in partnership with my husband, Harvy Lu, who is equally responsible for results produced. **Primary achievements:** Son Lee, 19, honor student at Harvard majoring in physics, state forensics champion. Daughter Su, 18, leading candidate for U.S. Olympic team in gymnastics, entering pre-law studies at the U of C, Berkeley. **Secondary achievements:** President of Piedmont High School PTA two years. Organized successful citizen protest to stop incursion of Oakland commercialism on Piedmont area.

PERSONAL DATA AND OTHER FACTS

Bachelor of Arts, Cody College, Cody, California. Highly active in community affairs. Have learned that there is a spark of genius in almost everyone, which, when nurtured, can flare into dramatic achievement.

(adapted from *Who's Hiring Who?* by Richard Lathrop, Ten Speed Press, 1987.)

Did you guess that Lili is a homemaker?

Combination Resume Example

Thomas Welborn

637 Wickham Road
Phoenix, AZ 85009

Home: (602) 253-9678
Leave Message: (602) 257-6643

JOB OBJECTIVE

Position in the electronics industry requiring skills in the design, sale, installation, maintenance, and repair of audio, video, and other advanced electronics. Prefer tasks needing creative problem-solving skills and customer contact.

EDUCATION

ITT TECHNICAL INSTITUTE
Phoenix, AZ
A.S. Degree,
Electronics Engineering Technology
1987-present

Completed a comprehensive, two-year curriculum including over 2000 hours of class and advanced laboratory. Theoretical, practical and hands-on knowledge of audio and RF amplifiers, AM/FM transmitter-receiver circuits, OP amplifiers, microwave and radar communications, digital circuits, and much more. Excellent attendance while working part time to pay tuition. Graduating in top 25 percent.

PLAINS JR. COLLEGE
Phoenix, AZ

Courses included digital electronics, programming, business, and computer applications. Worked full time and maintained a B+ average.

DESERT VIEW H.S.
1986 graduate

College prep. courses including advanced math, business, marketing, merchandising, computer orientation, and BASIC programming. Very active in varsity sports. National Junior Honor Society for two years.

Page 1

SKILLS

PROBLEM-SOLVING: Familiar with the underlying theory of most electronic systems and am particularly strong in isolating problems by using logic and persistence. I enjoy the challenge of solving complex problems and will work long hours, if necessary, to do this on a deadline.

INTERPERSONAL: Have supervised five staff and trained many more. Comfortable with one-to-one and small group communications. Can explain technical issues simply to customers of varying levels of sophistication. Had over 10,000 customer contacts in one job with no complaints and several written commendations.

TECHNICAL: Background in a variety of technical areas including medical equipment, consumer electronics, computers, automated cash registers, photocopiers, standard office and computer equipment and peripherals. Have designed special application combinational and sequential logic circuits using TTL logic. Constructed Z-80 microprocessor and wrote several machine language programs for this system. Can diagnose and repair problems in digital and analog circuits.

ORGANIZATIONAL: Have set up and run my own small business and worked in another responsible job while going to school full time. Earned enough money to live independently and pay all school expenses during this time. I can work independently and have learned to use my time efficiently.

EXPERIENCE

BANDLER'S INN: 1987-present. Waiter, promoted to night manager. Complete responsibility for all operations of a shift grossing over $300,000 in sales per year. Supervised five full-time and three part-time staff. Business increased during my employment by 35% and profits by 42%, much of it due to word of mouth advertising of satisfied customers.

FRANKLIN HOSPITAL: 1986-87. Electronic Service Technicians's Assistant. Worked in medical, physics, and electronics Departments. Assisted technicians in routine service and maintenance of a variety of hospital equipment. Part time while going to school.

TOM'S YARD SERVICE: 1984-1986. Set up a small business while in school. Worked part-time and summers doing yard work. Made enough money to buy a car and save for tuition.

Page 2

ACTIVITY Preparing A Superior Resume

Tips—Preparing A Superior Resume

- **Write it yourself.** It's okay to look at other resumes for ideas, but write yours yourself. It will force you to organize your thoughts and background.
- **Make it error free.** One spelling or grammar error will create a negative impression. Get someone else to review your final draft for any errors. Then review it again!
- **Make it look good.** Poor copy quality, cheap paper, bad type quality, or anything that creates a poor physical appearance will turn off employers.
- **Be brief, be relevant.** Many good resumes fit on one page; few justify more than two. Include only the most important points. Use short sentences and action words. If it doesn't relate to and support your job objective, take it out!
- **Be honest.** Don't overstate your qualifications. If you end up getting a job you can't handle, it will *not* be to your advantage.
- **Be positive.** Emphasize your accomplishments and results. This is no place to be too humble or to display your faults.
- **Be specific.** Rather than saying "I am good with people," say "I supervised four people in the warehouse and increased productivity by 30%." Use numbers whenever possible (people served, percentage increase, dollar increase, etc.).
- **Edit.** Write each of your resume drafts on a separate piece of paper. Make every word count. Keep editing until your resume is as good as you can make it. Then edit it again.
- **Use action words and short sentences.** Look at the sample resumes for ideas.
- **Avoid anything negative.** If an employer might consider anything in your resume as a negative, cut it out.

Tips—Having Your Resume Typed And Printed

- **Review resume.** Before you have the final typing done, be sure to have someone other than yourself, such as a teacher or counselor, review your resume.
- **Proper procedure.** Find out the procedures to follow to have your resume typed. Some high schools have them typed in one of the business classes.
- **Extra copies.** Get extra copies of your resume. Check with your teacher to see if your school allows you to make copies of your resume. Make sure that any copy you use is of excellent quality!
- **Custom Printing.** If possible, have your resume printed. Most "quick" print shops can handle this easily. Have them use a good quality ivory or buff color paper.

The Cover Letter

You should always include a cover letter or note when sending your resume to an employer. The cover letter should be brief, attract the employer's attention, and introduce you to the employer in a positive and professional way. The following is a sample cover letter to give you ideas for your own.

Sample Cover Letter

July 4, 1999

Ms. Janette King, Plant Manager
U.S. Machine Works
777 Pattern Way
Industrial City, California 54222

Dear Ms. King,

As promised in our recent phone conversation, I am sending you a copy of my resume. I was sorry that you could not interview me this week but want you to know that I am very interested in working for your organization.

I am young but do have experience. As part of my high school training, I have been enrolled in a business training program for the past two years. During that time, I have successfully learned to develop business plans, type, and use word processing equipment, and keep accounting records. My resume has details.

I am very interested in the possible job opening that you mentioned, and I would like to talk to you about it as soon as possible.

Please call me at any time. There are two phone numbers on my resume, and someone is at one of them most of the time. I will contact you again next week if I don't hear from you by then.

Sincerely,

Joseph Green

Joseph Green

Thank-You Notes and Letters

It is simply good manners to thank someone who has helped you during your job search. Send thank-you notes to employers who interview you and to others who help you in any way.

If your writing is neat, you can send a handwritten thank-you note. Most stationery and department stores have packages of printed thank-you notes and matching envelopes. This will help you present a professional appearance.

You may also send a typed thank-you letter. The following are examples of thank-you notes and letters.

Sample Thank-You Note

October 31, 1999

2234 Riverwood Ave.
Philadelphia, PA 17963

Ms. Helen A. Colcord
Henderson and Associates, Inc.
1801 Washington Blvd., Suite 1201
Philadelphia, PA 17963

Dear Ms. Colcord:

Thank you for sharing your time with me so generously today. I really appreciate seeing your state-of-the-art computer equipment.

Your advice has already proved helpful. I have an appointment to meet with Mr. Robert Hopper on Friday. As you anticipated, he does intend to add more computer operators in the next few months.

In case you think of someone else who might need a person like me, I'm enclosing another JIST Card. I will let you know how the interview with Mr. Hopper goes.

Sincerely,

William Richardson

William Richardson

Sample Thank-You Letter

February 14, 1999

Mr. Joseph Smith,
Assistant Plant Manager
J.J. Drill Company
44 Main Street
Acme, Ohio 54322

Dear Mr. Smith:

I would like to thank you for taking time to see me yesterday. I enjoyed talking to you about the prospects of working for your company.

The information you shared with me increased my interest and desire to work in such a setting. The job sounds very challenging, and I hope to be considered for this position.

Once again, thank you for taking time with me.

Sincerely,

John Valentine

John Valentine

Tips—Thank-You Notes And Letters

- **Thank-you letter.** You do not always have to send a formal, typed thank-you letter. A simple, neat, handwritten note can be just as effective.
- **Timing.** Send your note or letter as soon as possible after the interview or conversation.
- **Appearance counts!** Make sure that your note or letter is on good quality paper, is neat, and error free.

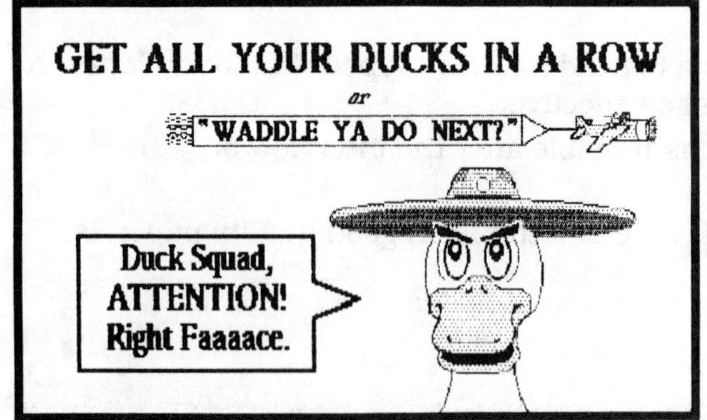

MEANWHILE:
In a dilapidated trainer plane high up above the unsuspecting Duck Squad, an emergency warning system notifies the unseasoned young pilot that **A FAIL-SAFE PLOT DEVICE HAS BEEN ACTIVATED!**

CONTINUED ON PAGE 105

CHAPTER 11

ORGANIZING YOUR JOB SEARCH

You are among that five percent of all job seekers who have had some sort of career search and job training. You have the inside track about many things people with better "credentials" do not have, and this will help you when it comes to getting job offers. The information in this chapter will help you organize the details necessary to make your job search a success and you a winner when you get the desired results.

The Objective Of Your Job Search: To Get Interviews

In order to get a job offer, you must get interviews. Before you learn how to organize your job search, let's review some important details.

The average job seeker gets about five interviews a month—fewer than two interviews a week. Yet many job seekers using JIST techniques find it easy to get two interviews a day! To do this, you have to redefine what an interview is. Here is our definition:

An Interview Is...

Face-to-face contact with anyone who has the authority to hire or supervise a person with your skills. They may or may not have a job opening at the time you have an interview with them.

With this definition, it is *much* easier to get interviews. You can now interview with all sorts of potential employers, not just those who have a job opening. Many job seekers use the *Yellow Pages* to get two interviews with just an hour of calls. They use the telephone contact script discussed earlier. Others simply drop in on potential employers and ask for an unscheduled interview. And they get them—not always, of course, but often enough.

Getting two interviews a day equals 10 a week and over 40 a month. That's 800% more interviews than the average job seeker gets. Who do you think will get a job offer more quickly?

Knowing and doing are two different things. So, your job at this time is to pull together what you have learned and make a plan of action.

ACTIVITY Let's Get Started! The Weekly Job Search Calendar

The first thing you need is a weekly job search calendar. It should include:

- The number of hours per week you plan to look for work.
- The days and hours you will look.
- The job search activities you will conduct during these times.

When completing your calendar, assume you are out of school, unemployed, and looking for a full-time job. In a real sense, you are scheduling your job as if it were a job itself. This calendar will become the "model" for your actual job search.

There are two parts to your calendar. The first helps you make basic decisions about your weekly schedule. The second shows you how to create your own sample calendar.

Part One: Basic Decisions

The average job seeker spends about five hours a week actually looking for work. They are also unemployed an average of three or more months! People who follow JIST's advice spend much more time on their job search each week. They also get jobs in less than half the average time—often much less than half. Let's get specific.

After you read each of the tips that follow, complete the relevant section of the Job Search Schedule Worksheet.

Tips—Completing The Job Search Schedule Worksheet

- **Hours per week.** Once you are out of school, how many hours per week do you plan to look for a job? We suggest at least 25 hours per week if you are unemployed and looking for a full time job. If 25 hours seems to be too many, select a number you feel sure you can keep. Write the number of hours on the worksheet.
- **Days.** What days will you look? Mondays through Fridays are the best days to look for most jobs, but weekends are good for some jobs, too. Put a check in the "yes" column of the worksheet for each day you plan to spend looking for a job.
- **How many hours each day?** You should decide in advance how many hours to spend on each of the days per week you will schedule for your job search. It is usually best to spend at least three or four hours on job search activities on each of the days you plan to look for work.
- **What times will you begin and end on each of these days?** The best times to contact most employers are from 8:00 a.m. to 5:00 p.m.
- **Notes.** Additional space has been provided for your thoughts and ideas as you fill in the Job Search Schedule Worksheet.

Job Search Schedule Worksheet

Days of Week	✔		Approximate # of Hours	Time Start/Stop	Actual # of Hours
	Yes	No			
Sunday	____	____	________	______to______	________
Monday	____	____	________	______to______	________
Tuesday	____	____	________	______to______	________
Wednesday	____	____	________	______to______	________
Thursday	____	____	________	______to______	________
Friday	____	____	________	______to______	________
Saturday	____	____	________	______to______	________
			Total # of Hours per Week ________		

Notes

Sunday ____

____

Monday ____

____

Tuesday ____

____

Wednesday ____

____

Thursday ____

____

Friday ____

____

Saturday ____

____

Part Two: Creating Your Weekly And Daily Job Search Calendar

You now need to decide *how* to spend your time each day. This is *very* important, since most job seekers find it hard to stay productive. You already know which job search methods are most effective, and you should plan to spend more of your time using these. The sample daily schedule which follows has been very effective for people who have used it and will give you ideas for your own schedule.

Sample Daily Job Search Schedule

Daily Schedule

7:00- 8:00 a.m.	Get up, shower, dress, eat breakfast, get ready to go to work!
8:00- 8:15 a.m.	Organize my work space; review schedule for interviews or promised follow-ups; update schedule as needed
8:15- 9:00 a.m.	Review old leads for follow-up; develop 20 new leads (want ads, Yellow Pages, networking lists, etc.)
9:00-10:00 a.m.	Make phone calls, set up interviews
10:00-10:15 a.m.	Take a break!
10:15-11:00 a.m.	Make more calls
11:00-12:00 p.m.	Make follow-up calls as needed
12:00- 1:00 p.m.	Lunch break
1:00- 3:00 p.m.	Go on interviews; make cold contacts in the field; research for interviews at the library

Now use the worksheet that follows to create your own daily schedule for a typical day. Use blank sheets of paper for extra worksheets as needed.

Daily Job Search Plan Worksheet

Day of Week____________________________

Time		Activity
Start	End	

Notes

Day of Week____________________________

Time		Activity
Start	End	

Notes

Day of Week____________________________

Time		Activity
Start	End	

Notes

Weekly Job Search Schedule Worksheet

Use the information you developed in this chapter to create a schedule for a typical week of looking for work. Look at the following sample, then make your own on the blank worksheet.

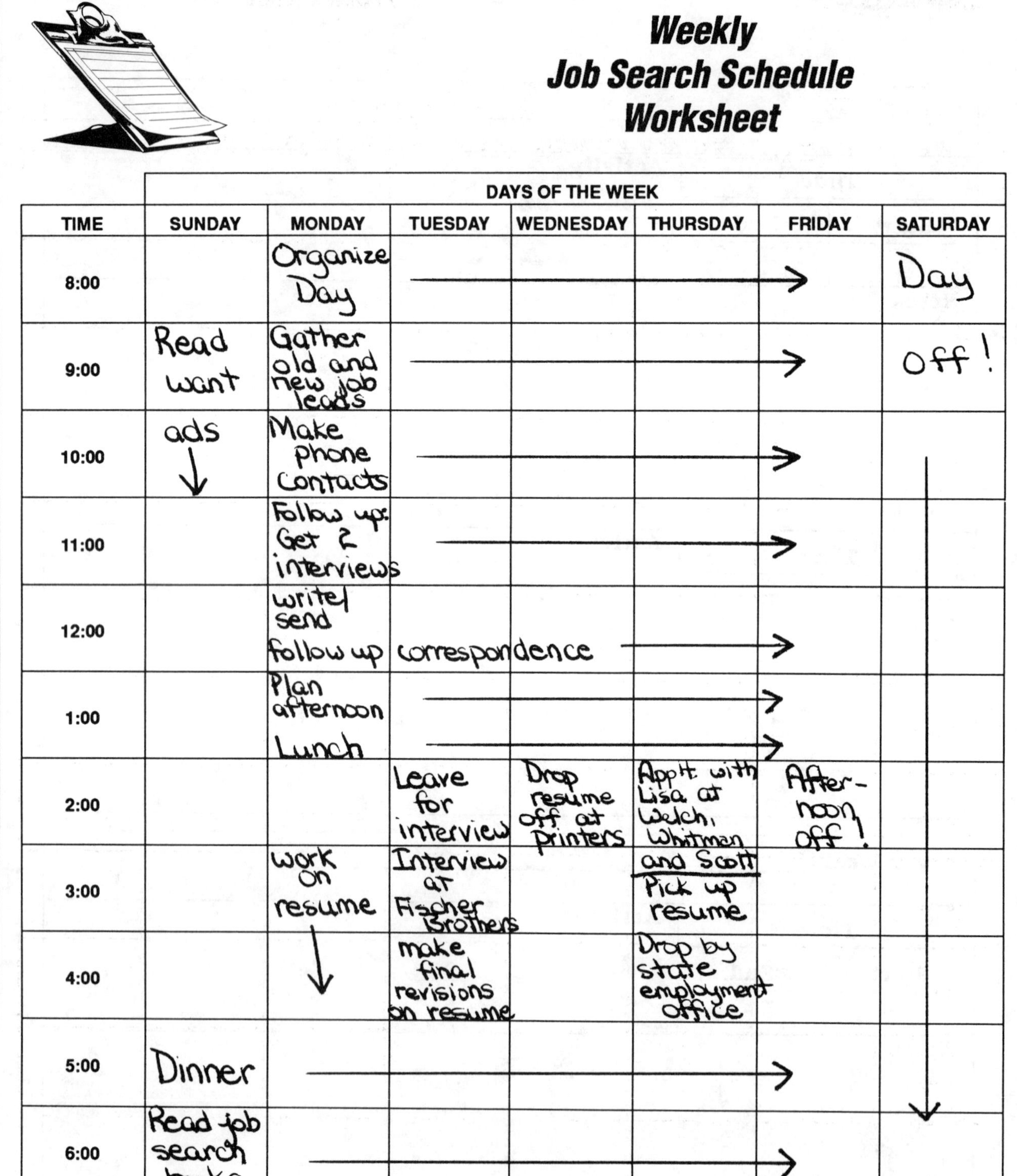

Weekly Job Search Schedule Worksheet

	DAYS OF THE WEEK						
TIME	**SUNDAY**	**MONDAY**	**TUESDAY**	**WEDNESDAY**	**THURSDAY**	**FRIDAY**	**SATURDAY**
8:00		Organize Day	→	→	→		Day
9:00	Read want	Gather old and new job leads	→	→	→		Off!
10:00	ads ↓	Make phone contacts	→	→	→		↓
11:00		Follow up: Get 2 interviews	→	→	→		
12:00		write/ send follow up	correspondence	→	→		
1:00		Plan afternoon Lunch	→ →	→ →	→ →		
2:00			Leave for interview	Drop resume off at printers	Appt with Lisa at Welch, Whitman and Scott	After-noon off!	
3:00		work on resume	Interview at Fischer Brothers		Pick up resume		
4:00		↓	make final revisions on resume		Drop by state employment office		
5:00	Dinner	→	→	→	→		
6:00	Read job search books	→	→	→	→		

Weekly Job Search Schedule Worksheet

	DAYS OF THE WEEK						
TIME	SUNDAY	MONDAY	TUESDAY	WEDNESDAY	THURSDAY	FRIDAY	SATURDAY
8:00							
9:00							
10:00							
11:00							
12:00							
1:00							
2:00							
3:00							
4:00							
5:00							
6:00							

Tips—Completing Your Weekly Schedule

Your goal is to get interviews! Try to reach that goal in steps. Strive for:

- Three to four interviews during the first week.
- At least one interview a day during the second week.
- Two interviews a day during the third and additional weeks. Keep going until success comes your way and you get the job you want.

JIST Job Search Course Review

Here is a review of *the basics* for getting the job you want. The blank space after each section is provided for your thoughts as you think about the following statements.

1. **Know what job you want.**
   - Do not ask for just "any job you have."
   - Why do you want the job?
   - What skills do you have to do it well?
   - What is the salary range for this type of job?
   - What other jobs require similar skills?

   ____

   ____

   ____

2. **Know what the employer is looking for.**
   - Are you a good, hard worker?
   - Can the employer depend on you—to be on time, have good attendance, and do the job?
   - Do you seem to really want this job—and say so?
   - If you don't have the best experience, can you overcome this?
   - Will you stay with the organization?
   - Will you be sick or injured?
   - Do your good points outweigh your weaknesses?

   ____

   ____

   ____

3. **Know where to look.**
   - Small businesses hire about 2/3 of all people—look for them!
   - Spend more time with the most effective job search methods: networking and direct contacts with employers.
   - Network with friends, relatives, and acquaintances for job leads and for names of other people to contact.
   - Use the *Yellow Pages* to find and contact large and small employers.

- Use traditional job lead sources, too: want ads, state employment service, and others.
- Investigate federal, state, county, city, and other government and not-for-profit organizations.

4. **Know how to look.**
   - Always apply alone.
   - Organize. Apply at several places in the same area.
   - Send thank-you notes.
   - Stay in touch with employers and anyone who might help you get job leads.
   - Use the phone to save time in setting up interviews and in following up.
   - Get lots of interviews—even if there is no job open now, be considered for future ones.
   - Follow up on all interviews. If you want the job, say so.

5. ***Think.***
   - You have abilities and skills that some employer needs.
   - Learn from your failures as well as your successes.
   - Find out the reasons you were turned down and overcome them in the next interview.
   - If you can't get one type of job, look for another.
   - Don't be afraid of asking questions. If you don't know something, ask.

6. **Keep trying.**
   - You must apply for work to get it.
   - There are openings every day for most skills—though they may be hard to find!
   - Make your job search into a job itself.
   - Spend at least 25 hours a week looking for work.
   - Set your goal at getting two interviews a day.
   - Don't give up on yourself. You are a good person, and you will survive long enough to get your next job.

A Formula For Job Search Success

Here is a simple formula for getting a good job:

Yellow Pages + Networking + Cold Contacts = Job Leads

Job Leads + Telephone Contacts = Interviews

Interviews = Job Offers

Job Offers = ***A JOB!***

CONTINUED FROM PAGE 94

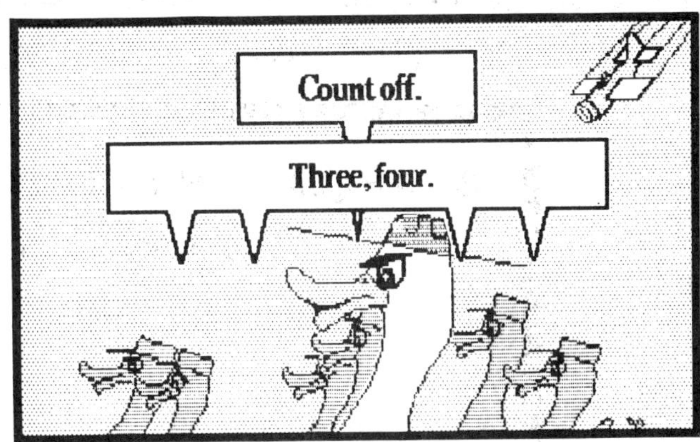

GREAT MOMENTS IN CLASSICAL MYTHOLOGY

Chapter 13: Perseus and Medusa

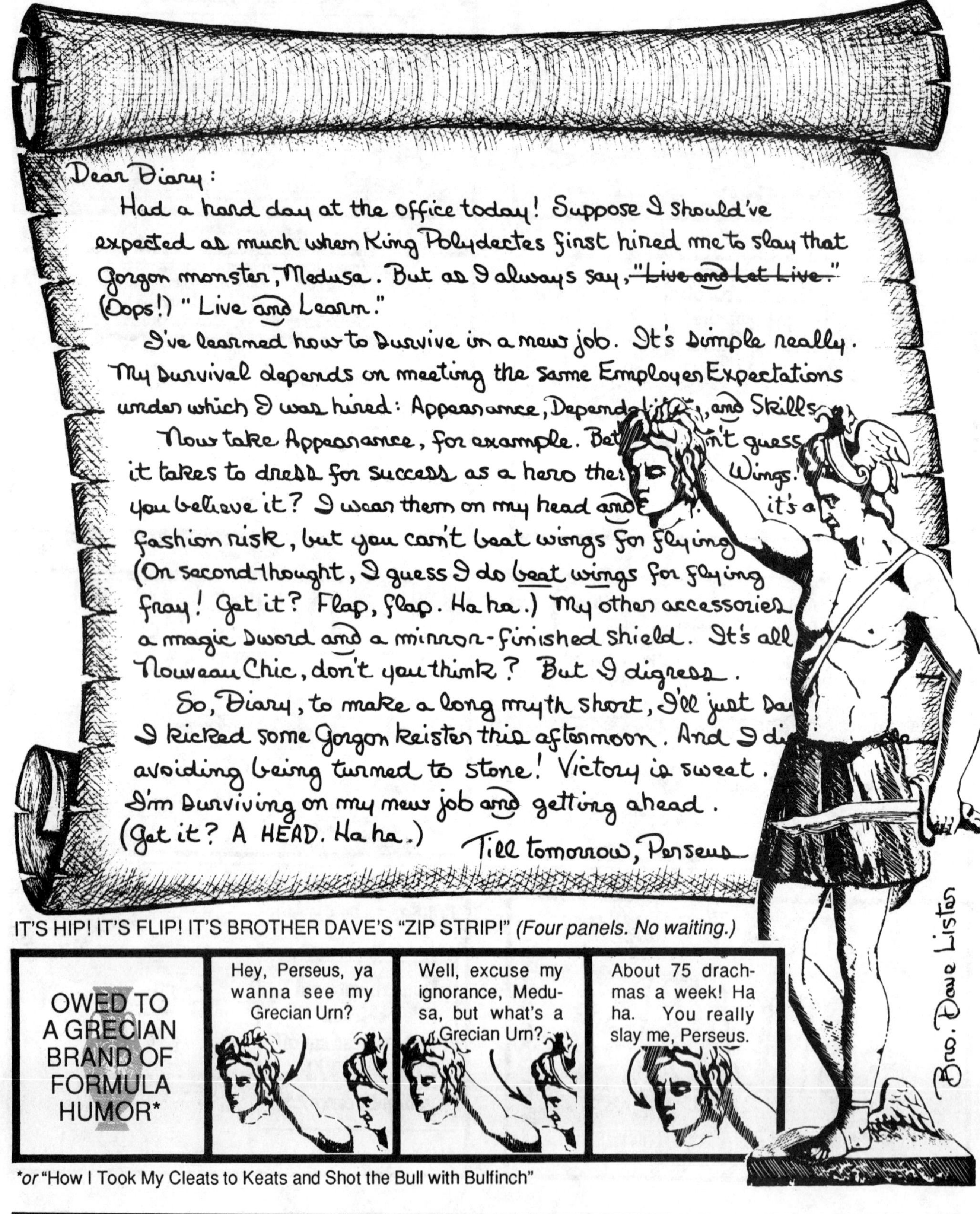

*or "How I Took My Cleats to Keats and Shot the Bull with Bulfinch"

CHAPTER 12

SURVIVING ON A NEW JOB AND GETTING AHEAD

During the years you work you will have many different jobs. Each new job will bring about changes in your life, and each one will present chances to learn and problems to overcome. This chapter was written to help you get off to a successful start.

Success On The Job

As you begin a new job, you will probably feel a bit of fear, because you don't know what to expect. Will you get along with the other people who work there? Are you dressed right? Will you be able to handle the new responsibilities?

ACTIVITY Getting Off To A Good Start—Employer Expectations

You were hired because the employer felt that you had the skills and abilities needed to get the job done. You will now be expected to become a productive employee. Now is your chance to prove that you really do meet all three major employer expectations: *appearance, dependability, and skills.*

Appearance

Here are some things to consider when beginning a new job:

- **Self-Image.** Show confidence in the way you present yourself.
- **Dress.** Be neat and clean in your appearance and grooming. Dress appropriately for the type of job you are starting.

- **Personality.** Be natural, friendly, and show respect to your co-workers and supervisors. Don't forget to smile!
- **Communications.** Use good verbal skills when you talk to others. Show your interest by asking questions and being positive.
- **Behavior.** Be cooperative with others, and work hard at adjusting to the work routine expected of you. Find a "buddy" to help you learn the basics of the job.

Ways I Can Improve

Select three items of appearance, either from the list above or others not included, that you feel you can improve. For each, write a self-improvement activity that will help you be successful on the job.

1. Item:____________________ Ways I can improve: ____________________

2. Item:____________________ Ways I can improve: ____________________

3. Item:____________________ Ways I can improve: ____________________

Dependability

One way to prove that you are worthy of your new job is to show that you are dependable. All employers *expect* you to be dependable. Make the following a natural part of your daily job habits:

- **Be at work on time.** Arrive a few minutes early. Allow yourself enough travel time, considering the traffic situation and the route you will take.
- **Follow the expected work schedule.** Take only the time allowed for breaks and lunch. Be sure to arrive back at your workstation on the scheduled time or a few minutes early.
- **Know what duties you should be performing.** Be sure that you complete what is expected of you. Ask your supervisor to explain any special procedures or rules to

you. Ask for and read at home any personnel and procedure materials related to your job.

- **Don't miss work.** A minor illness (like a cold) is not a good reason for missing work, nor are most personal problems (such as child care). If you miss more than three days a year for these reasons, it may be too much.
- **Call if you will be absent or late.** If you will be more than a few minutes late or absent for any reason, call in at the beginning of the work day. Talk directly to your supervisor and explain the situation. Do not leave a message. Sometimes, you may be able to call the day before if you think there could be a problem.

Ways I Can Improve

Select three items indicating that you are dependable, either from the list above or others that are not included. For each, write a self-improvement activity that will help you be successful on the job.

1. Item:________________ Ways I can improve: ________________

2. Item:________________ Ways I can improve: ________________

3. Item:________________ Ways I can improve: ________________

Skills

Your performance on the job will show the employer whether or not he or she made the right choice in hiring you. How well will you measure up?

- **Show that you do have the skills.** And then apply them daily.
- **Strive to improve your skills.** Develop new ways to do a better job.
- **Seek ways to learn new skills.** Learn all you can from any job you have. Do the job as well as you are able. Look for ways to spend your time more efficiently.
- **Accept responsibility.** For your job and your performance on the job.

- **Work fast but carefully.** It is important to work at a steady and quick pace. Find a pace that you can keep up all day without making errors.
- **Be willing to take on additional responsibilities.** Try your best to do something "extra" when you are asked. Volunteer for tasks that allow you to learn something new.

Ways I Can Improve

Select three items either from the list above or others not included that you feel you can improve. For each, write a self-improvement activity that will help you be successful on the job.

1. Item:____________________ Ways I can improve: ____________________

2. Item:____________________ Ways I can improve: ____________________

3. Item:____________________ Ways I can improve: ____________________

Other Expectations

- **Stay away from "problem" employees.** Some people tend to be negative about their jobs. Others do things against the rules, waste time, or in other ways are not good workers. They may even be fun to be with. But spending time with them will affect your performance. Your co-workers and supervisors may begin to see *you* as a "problem." Be friendly, but do not socialize with people like this any more than is necessary.
- **Keep personal problems at home.** You are paid to get a job done. Making personal phone calls, paying bills, coming back late from lunch, or talking to other staff about what you did last weekend are not what you are being paid to do. Although some socializing on the job is common, you can easily overdo it. Limit your personal activities and discussions to breaks, lunch times, or hours outside of work.
- **Children and other family members.** Although children or other family members may be the most important part of your life, they are not the concern of an employer.

Make sure that child care arrangements are in place prior to accepting a job. If your children are in school, arrange child care so that you do not miss work when they are ill. Strongly discourage personal phone calls except in emergencies. When interviewing for a job, tell employers that you will be a dependable worker and that child care has been arranged. Assure them that you needn't miss work for this reason.

Ways I Can Improve

Select three of the items either from the expectations list above or others not included. For each, write a self-improvement activity that will help you be successful on the job.

1. Item:____________________ Ways I can improve: ____________________

   ____

   ____

   ____

   ____

2. Item:____________________ Ways I can improve: ____________________

   ____

   ____

   ____

   ____

3. Item:____________________ Ways I can improve: ____________________

   ____

   ____

   ____

   ____

Why People Get Fired

Everyone wants to be accepted and successful on a new job. Surviving on the job may mean that you have to change the way you act and some of your attitudes. To get ideas on how to succeed on a new job, let's consider the employer's point of view.

In the spaces below, list the top three reasons you think an employer would have for firing someone.

1. ____
2. ____
3. ____

The Reasons People Are Fired: The Employer's Point Of View

One way to survive on a job is to make sure that you avoid the things that get people fired. Here are the top 10 reasons employers give for firing people. The top 3 are listed first. Compare your answers with the real ones!

- **Was dishonest.** This is one of the top reasons employers give for firing someone. More employers are now screening new applicants to eliminate people who have been dishonest with previous employers. Employers don't want to pay someone who steals from them or can't be trusted.
- **Worked too slowly.** This is a major reason for job failure. You can see why: unproductive employees cost more than they earn! A slow worker is expensive compared to another worker who gets the same job done in less time.
- **Would not follow orders; did not get along with supervisor.** In a battle with a supervisor, you will almost always lose!
- **Was unreliable; too many days absent or late.** When an employee is absent, it disrupts the work of other people. They may have to neglect their work to make up for the absent worker. Being late sets a bad example for others and often disrupts the work of other people.
- **Could not get along with other workers.** Many workers consider this problem one of the top reasons they don't like their jobs. While few employers list it among the very top reasons for firing someone, it is often a factor. You don't have to like all the people you work with, but it is important that you get along with them.
- **Dressed or groomed poorly.** The way you look is very important. This is particularly true in office jobs and in jobs where you deal with customers. Poor dress and grooming affect how the employer feels about you. This can be one of many things a terminated employee did not do well.
- **Made too many mistakes.** Someone who makes mistakes can be costly to an employer in many ways. Perhaps another employee has to spend time correcting errors. A customer may become unhappy with the company's products or services as a result of sloppy work. That customer doesn't come back—and tells others not to do so.
- **Had too many accidents; did not follow safety rules.** Employers do not want to keep people who have accidents or who do not follow safety rules. Accidents can be costly to employers and dangerous to other employees.
- **Could not do the work.** Few people get fired because they could not do the work. Employers tend to hire people they think can do the job and then give them time to learn it.
- **Abused alcohol or drugs.** Substance abuse is a major problem in some organizations. A person who abuses alcohol or drugs often gets fired for being unreliable or for some other reason. The employer may not even know the cause of the problem.

There are many reasons an employer might fire a person. Almost any reason can be enough if it is a serious problem. More often, however, people are fired for more than one reason. For example, they may be late to work too often and make too many mistakes in their work. Perhaps you know of someone who was fired. What were the reasons?

____

____

____

It's Not Always Your Fault

Most people will get fired one or more times in their careers. Often, it has nothing to do with what you did—such as when a business closes. You can even do a good job but have a personality conflict with your boss or other workers. Such people often find new jobs where they do much better.

There are many reasons people lose or leave their jobs. If this happens to you, it is important to learn from the experience and to look for a new job that does not present the same problems.

Advanced Tips—Moving Up The Career Ladder

Once you settle into the routine of your new job, some questions will occur to you:

- Can I continue to meet the employer's expectations?
- Do I really like what I am doing?
- What will it take to be promoted?
- How can I have more control over the job?

You may answer these and other questions by forming some additional work habits. Use the space following each tip to write notes on how you can best use them.

Getting Ahead

1. **Dress and groom for a promotion.**
   - If you want to get ahead in an organization, dress and groom as if you work at the level you hope to reach next. This is not always possible, but at the very least, be clean and well groomed.
   - Wear clothes that fit well and look good on you. Copy the clothing styles of others who are successful in the organization. Even when your co-workers see you away from work, present the image you want for yourself at work.

   ____

   ____

   ____

   ____

2. **Be early and stay late.**
   - Get to work a few minutes early each day. Use this time to list what you plan to get done that day. At the end of the day, leave a few minutes after quitting time.
   - Be willing to stay late to meet an important deadline. If you do stay late, let the boss know! Unless you are asked though, stay late only when you have an important deadline to meet.

   ____

   ____

   ____

   ____

3. Be enthusiastic.

- Go out of your way to find ways to enjoy your job. Tell others what you like about it, particularly those you work with. Emphasize those parts of your job that you like to do and do well. Share this enthusiasm even in conversations with your friends.
- Make a particular effort to tell your supervisor what you like about your job. This will help you focus on the parts of your job you are most likely to want to do more of. It will also help others notice that you do them well.

____

____

____

____

4. Ask for more responsibility.

- As soon as you begin a new job, look for ways to learn new things. Volunteer to help out in ways you feel will make you more valuable to the organization. Let the boss know you want to move up. Ask for advice about what you can do to be more valuable to the organization.

____

____

____

____

5. Ask how you can earn more money.

- In your first week on the job, ask your supervisor to see you for about 30 minutes of private time. When you have his or her attention, say that you want to be more valuable to the organization. Ask what you can do to get a raise as soon as possible. Request special assignments to help develop your skills.
- Before you leave the meeting, ask for a specific future date to go over your progress and what you have to do to get the raise. Ask the boss to give you feedback on your progress from time to time.

____

____

____

____

6. Ask for training.

- Get as much training as possible! Even if it is outside of your job responsibilities, request the training the organization provides if it sounds at all useful or interesting.

- Define the type of training you need to do your job better, and look for it outside the organization. Explain to your supervisor how the training will help the organization. Ask for help in finding the best training source.

____

____

____

____

7. **Take on difficult projects.**

- You won't get much attention unless you do more than is expected of you. Look for projects that you think you can do well and that would benefit the organization in some clear way.
- Don't promise too much and keep a low profile while you do the work. If no one expects too much, it is easier to be seen as successful, even if your results are not as good as you had hoped.

____

____

____

8. **Get measurable results.**

- Keep records of what you do. Compare them to past performance or the average performance of others in similar situations. If your results look good, send a report to your supervisor. For example, if the number of orders went up 40 percent over the same month last year with no increase in staff, that's a big accomplishment. Look for ways to present what you do in numbers, such as dollars saved, percentage of increased sales, number of persons served, number of units processed, and size of budget.

____

____

____

____

Leaving A Job

Many of you have held part-time jobs in the past and may work at one now. Even if you have never worked, you do need to learn how to leave a job. Here are some tips:

- **Don't just quit:** If the job is not working out for you, ask for a job change within the organization before you give up. If you are unhappy about your job, *do not* talk about it to anyone who works with you until you have found another job. Some people have lost their jobs when their boss finds out they are unhappy or planning to leave.

- **Look for another job before quitting.** If possible, begin your job search while you are still employed. You can update your resume, set up interviews before or after work, or take vacation time off to look.
- **Notify your employer:** Once you decide to leave, give 30 days notice if at all possible. Two weeks notice is the minimum you should give.
- **Give a written notice:** A formal letter of resignation should be given to your supervisor when you tell him or her, in person, that you are leaving. Stress the positive experiences you had and the good feelings you have about the people you worked with.
- **Complete all responsibilities related to your job:** This is especially important if you are working on an individual project or as part of a team effort. Be prepared to train a new person in your job.
- **Ask for a letter of reference:** Make this request to your supervisor before you leave. If you did well, the letter will be positive, and it is much easier to get it now. If there were problems, at least you will know what he or she will say about you to future employers!

Sample Resignation Letter

Here is a sample letter you can use as a guide in preparing your own.

February 2, 1999

Anne Marie Rhodes
Assistant Plant Manager
J.J. Drill Company
44 Main Street
Los Angeles, California 54322

Dear Ms. Rhodes,

It has been a very valuable experience working for you, but I have been offered a job with another organization and have accepted their offer. I feel that this position will give me the experience I need to move up in my career. Therefore, I will be resigning my job 30 days from today.

I would like to express my thanks for your personal interest in me, and I want you to know that I will miss everyone I have worked with since I have been here.

Sincerely,

David Abeel

David Abeel

Remember

It is far better to leave on a positive note with your present employer and co-workers. Don't forget that many employers *do* check work references, and you want to be sure that only good things will be said about you.

In Conclusion

You know much more about looking for work than most people your age. While this book ends here, there is so much more to come. We offer you a few final lessons in closing:

- **Don't be afraid to try things.** You will probably have many jobs during the years ahead, some good, some not so good. Each one will teach you something and help you in some way for what is to come.
- **Decide to do something worthwhile.** Whether it is raising a family or saving the whales, believe in something you do as special, as lasting, as valuable.
- **Work well.** All work is worth doing, so put your energy into it, and do it as well as you are able.
- **Enjoy life.** It's sort of the same as having fun, but it lasts longer and means more.
- **Send thank-you notes.** Many people will help you throughout your life, in large and small ways. Let them know you appreciate them. The more you give, the more you seem to get in return.

We wish you good fortune in your job search and your life!

Addendum: Getting Career Information—Figuring Out A Job Objective

Exploring Careers

This book assumes that you already have a good idea of the kind of job you want. If you do, this section can give you additional information on learning about the many types of jobs in your career area.

If you are not sure what you want to do after high school, that is okay, too. Most young people will try a variety of jobs before they settle into one job or career area. You may also need to earn some money while going to school or feel that you just want to "goof off" awhile before getting serious about working.

Whatever your situation, it is to your advantage to know how to find out about the many careers available and to concentrate on the ones that seem most interesting.

There are over 20,000 jobs listed by the U.S. Department of Labor. That is far more than you can hope to learn about during this course. There are many ways to approach career exploration. Here are some of the most useful:

Counseling Resources

Career Counseling

Your school is often a good source of information and advice. Make sure you know what services are available and use them!

Testing Resources

There are a variety of vocational tests you can take to help you learn more about your interests and abilities. Following are brief comments on the most popular types.

Interest Tests

Interest tests allow you to compare the things that interest you to what is done in various careers. The tests we recommend are those that allow you to learn about various career clusters as a part of completing the test.

Two tests of this kind that we recommend are the Self Directed Search (SDS) and The Career Decision Making System (CDM). They are both self-scoring and very helpful in selecting a career area for more exploration. The SDS is published by Psychological Assessment Resources in Odessa, Florida, and the CDM is published by the American Guidance Service, Circle Pines, Minnesota. (Both of these tests are also available to schools—not individual students—from JIST, the publisher of this book.)

Ability Tests

These tests are quite different in that they compare what you know and what you can do to the skills of people who already work in various fields. A carpenter, for example, needs to be good with his or her hands and to be able to use various measuring tools. If you do well on the test in manual dexterity and basic math, the test might suggest that carpentry is one of the fields you could do well in. You might hate working with your hands, but the test doesn't consider this.

Two good abilities tests are the General Abilities Test Battery (GATB) and the Armed Services Vocational Test Battery (ASVAB). Most local employment service offices can give you the GATB if you ask them, and you can arrange to take the ASVAB at most recruiting offices of the armed services. Neither one charges a fee, and the information you get can be very helpful. Of course, you will get a pitch to join the armed forces if you take the ASVAB, but you can always say "no" (though in some cases saying "yes" can be a very good decision).

Other Tests

Your school counselor may have other tests available, and all of them can be helpful in some way. But tests are not magic. They can't give you final answers and are often incomplete. You should trust your own sense of what is right for you and do that. Tests can be wrong, and there are many people out here doing things the tests said we wouldn't be good at—and enjoying it. So trust yourself above all else.

Printed Resources

The Library

There are many good books, journals, and other materials on many careers in most libraries. Check your school library for what it has on a career you are interested in. Also ask the librarian at the public library for a source of journals and magazines that people who work in the career you are interested in would read. These are an excellent source of information on what is going on in that occupation.

The *Occupational Outlook Handbook (OOH)*

We consider this one of the most helpful sources of career information available. Most school counseling offices have one of these books, as do most libraries. Published by the U.S. Department of Labor, it lists about 200 of the most popular jobs in the country—2/3 of all people work in one of these. It is updated every two years, so try to get the most current edition.

The jobs are organized into clusters of related occupations. This makes it easy to find ones that seem interesting and to consider ones requiring similar skills that you may not have considered before. The description for each job includes information on working conditions, future openings, related jobs, pay scales, training required, and other details. Because it is updated every two years, the information is current, and the descriptions are very well done.

A list of jobs covered in the *OOH* is at the end of this section. Look up the jobs you are interested in, and read about them in the *OOH*. Schools can obtain copies of the *OOH* from JIST.

The *Guide For Occupational Exploration (GOE)*

Also published by the Department of Labor, the *GOE* provides a helpful method of exploring careers based on interests, previous experience, skills, and other factors. The improved second edition (published by JIST) has useful activities to help define occupational interests and other features. Many libraries have a copy of the first edition, but the newer second edition is harder to find.

Exploring Careers

Exploring Careers, written specifically for high school aged students, provides a series of worksheets and activities to hep you explore career alternatives. It also provides information on over 300 jobs and gives an "insiders view" of what it is like to work on various jobs. Originally published by the U.S. Department of Labor, it was completely revised in 1990 and is available from JIST.

Human Resources

Other People

Much of what you already know about various jobs has come from other people. Ask your parents and others what they do and do not like about their jobs. Then compare this to your own likes and dislikes. Ask questions of people you meet who work in different jobs. When you identify a job that really interests you, find someone who does that kind of work for a living, and ask them to tell you more about it.

Entry Level and Volunteer Jobs

Many young people can get jobs in areas they are interested in as careers. If you want to work in the medical field, for example, try to get a job in a hospital or other medical facility. Hospitals are also one example of a place that often uses volunteers in various roles, and you can often use this unpaid experience to get a paid job doing related tasks.

Working Your Way Up

You may have to start at the bottom and work your way up. Young people can often take an entry-level job and use it to show that they can work hard and be trusted.

For example, if you have never managed a business, few employers would hire you to run one. But you might be able to get a job as a stock clerk, and then learn as much as possible about the business. Let the employer know that you want more responsibility, and be willing to take on new tasks. Even if you can't move up in that job, you can use what you learn to get a better one in the future.

Occupational Outlook Handbook Occupations Listing

Managerial and Management-Related Occupations
- Accountants and auditors
- Construction and building inspectors
- Cost estimators
- Education administrators
- Employment interviewers
- Financial managers
- General managers and top executives
- Health services managers
- Hotel managers and assistants
- Inspectors and compliance officers, except construction
- Management analysts and consultants
- Marketing, advertising, and public relations managers
- Personnel, training, and labor relations specialists and managers
- Property and real estate managers
- Purchasing agents and managers
- Restaurant and food service managers
- Underwriters
- Wholesale and retail buyers

Engineers, Surveyors, and Architects

Engineers
- Aerospace engineers
- Chemical engineers
- Civil engineers
- Electrical and electronics engineers
- Industrial engineers
- Mechanical engineers
- Metallurgical, ceramic, and materials engineers
- Mining engineers
- Nuclear engineers
- Petroleum engineers

Architects and surveyors
- Architects
- Landscape architects
- Surveyors

Natural, Computer, and Mathematical Scientists

Computer, mathematical, and operations research occupations
- Actuaries
- Computer systems analysts
- Mathematicians
- Operations research analysts
- Statisticians

Life scientists
- Agricultural scientists
- Biological scientists
- Foresters and conservation scientists

Physical scientists
- Chemists
- Geologists and geophysicists
- Meteorologists
- Physicists and astronomers

Lawyers, Social Scientists, Social Workers, and Religious Workers
- Lawyers

Social scientists and urban planners
- Economists
- Psychologists
- Sociologists
- Urban and regional planners

Social and recreation workers
- Human services workers
- Social workers
- Recreation workers

Religious Workers
- Protestant ministers
- Rabbis
- Roman Catholic priests

Teachers, Librarians, and Counselors
- Adult and vocational education teachers
- Archivists and curators
- College and university faculty
- Counselors
- Kindergarten and elementary school teachers
- Librarians
- Secondary school teachers

Health Diagnosing and Treating Practitioners
- Chiropractors
- Dentists
- Optometrists
- Physicians
- Podiatrists
- Veterinarians

Registered Nurses, Pharmacists, Dietitians, Therapists and Physician Assistants
- Dietitians and nutritionists
- Occupational therapists
- Pharmacists
- Physical therapists

Physician assistants
Recreational therapists
Registered nurses
Respiratory therapists
Speech-language pathologists and audiologists

Health Technologists and Technicians
Clinical laboratory technologists and technicians
Dental hygienists
Dispensing opticians
EEG technologists and technicians
EKG technicians
Emergency medical technicians
Licensed practical nurses
Medical record technicians
Nuclear medicine technologists
Radiologic technologists
Surgical technicians

Writers, Artists, and Entertainers
Communications occupations
Public relations specialists
Radio and television announcers and newscasters
Reporters and correspondents
Writers and editors
Visual arts occupations
Designers
Photographers and camera operators
Visual artists
Performing arts occupations
Actors, directors, and producers
Dancers and choreographers
Musicians

Technologists and Technicians, Except Health
Air traffic controllers
Broadcast technicians
Computer programmers
Drafters
Engineering technicians
Legal assistants
Library technicians
Science technicians
Tool programmers, numerical control

Marketing and Sales Occupations
Cashiers
Counter and rental clerks
Insurance sales workers
Manufacturers' sales workers
Real estate agents and brokers
Retail sales workers
Securities and financial services sales representatives
Services sales representatives
Travel agents
Wholesale trade sales workers

Administrative Support Occupations, Including Clerical
Bank tellers
Bookkeepers and accounting clerks
Clerical supervisors and managers
Computer and peripheral equipment operators
Data entry keyers
File clerks
General office clerks
Insurance claims and policy processing occupations
Postal clerks and mail carriers
Receptionists and information clerks
Reservation and transportation ticket agents and travel clerks
Secretaries
Statistical clerks
Stenographers
Stock clerks
Teacher aides
Telephone operators
Traffic, shipping, and receiving clerks
Typists and word processors

Service Occupations
Protective service occupations
Correction officers
Firefighting occupations
Guards
Police, detectives, and special agents
Food and beverage preparation and service occupations
Chefs, cooks, and other kitchen workers
Food and beverage service occupations
Health service occupations
Dental assistants
Medical assistants
Nursing aides and psychiatric aides
Personal service and cleaning occupations
Barbers
Childcare workers
Cosmetologists and related workers
Flight attendants
Homemaker-home health aides
Janitors and cleaners
Private household workers

Agriculture, Forestry, Fishery, and Related Occupations
Farm operators and managers
Timber cutting and logging occupations

Mechanics, Installers, and Repairers
Aircraft mechanics and engine specialists
Automotive body repairers
Automotive mechanics
Commerical and industrial electronic euipment repairers
Communications equipment mechanics
Computer service technicians
Diesel mechanics
Electronic home entertainment equipment repairers
Elevator installers and repairers
Farm equipment mechanics
General maintenance mechanics
Heating, air-conditioning, and refrigeration mechanics
Home applicance and power tool repairers
Industrial machinery repairers
Line installers and cable splicers
Millwrights
Mobile heavy equipment mechanics
Motorcycle, boat, and small-engine mechanics
Musical instrument repairers and tuners
Office machine and cash register servicers
Telephone installers and repairers
Vending machine servicers and repairers

Construction Trades and Extractive Occupations
Bricklayers and stonemasons
Carpenters
Carpet installers
Concrete masons and terrazzo workers
Drywall workers and lathers
Electricians
Glaziers
Insulation workers
Painters and paperhangers
Plasterers
Plumbers and pipefitters
Roofers
Roustabouts
Sheet-metal workers
Structural and reinforcing metal workers
Tilesetters

Production Occupations
Apparel workers
Bindery workers
Blue-collar worker supervisors
Boilermakers
Butchers and meatcutters
Compositors and typesetters
Dental laboratory technicians
Electric power generating plant operators and power distributors and dispatchers
Inspectors, testers, and graders
Jewelers
Lithographic and photoengraving workers
Machinists
Metalworking and plastic-working machine operators
Numerical-control machine-tool operators
Ophthalmic laboratory technicians
Painting and coating machine operators
Photographic process workers
Precision assemblers
Printing press operators
Shoe and leather workers and repairers
Stationary engineers
Textile machinery operators
Tool-and-die makers
Upholsterers
Water and wastewater treatment plant operators
Welders, cutters, and welding machine operators
Woodworking occupations

Transportation and Material Moving Occupations
Aircraft pilots
Busdrivers
Material moving equipment operators
Truckdrivers

Handlers, Equipment Cleaners, Helpers, and Laborers
Construction trades helpers

Job Opportunities in the Armed Forces
Military

Other Titles Available From

JIST publishes a variety of books on careers and job search topics. Please consider ordering one or more from your dealer, local bookstore, or directly from JIST.

Orders from individuals: Please use the form below (or provide the same information) to order additional copies of this or other books listed on this page. You are also welcome to send us your order (please enclose money order or check) or, if paying with a credit card, simply call our toll free number at **1-800-648-JIST** or **1-317-264-3720**. Our FAX number is **1-317-264-3709**. **Qualified schools and organizations** may request our catalog and obtain information on quantity discounts (we have over 400 career-related books, videos, software, and other items). Our offices are open weekdays 8 a.m. to 5 p.m. local time and our address is:

JIST Works, Inc. • 720 North Park Avenue • Indianapolis, IN 46202-3431

QUANTITY	BOOK TITLE	TOTAL($)
______	***Getting the Job You Really Want***, J. Michael Farr • ISBN: 0-942784-15-4 • **$9.95**	______
______	***The Very Quick Job Search:*** *Get a Good Job in Less Time*, J. Michael Farr • ISBN 0-942784-72-3 • **$9.95**	______
______	***America's 50 Fastest Growing Jobs:*** *An Authoritative Information Source* • ISBN 0-942784-61-8 • **$9.95**	______
______	***America's Top 300 Jobs:*** *A Complete Career Handbook* (trade version of the *Occupational Outlook Handbook*) • ISBN 0-942784-826-X • **$17.95**	______
______	***America's Federal Jobs:*** *A Complete Directory of Federal Career Opportunities* • ISBN 0-942784-81-2 • **$14.95**	______
______	***The Resume Solution:*** *How to Write and Use a Resume That Gets Results*, David Swanson • ISBN 942784-44-8 • **$10.95**	______
______	***The Job Doctor:*** *Good Advice on Getting a Good Job*, Dr. Phillip Norris, Ph.D. • ISBN 0-942784-43-X • **$8.95**	______
______	***The Right Job for You:*** *An Interactive Career Planning Guide*, J. Michael Farr • ISBN 0-942784-73-1 • **$9.95**	______
______	***Exploring Careers:*** *A Young Person's Guide to over 300 Jobs* • ISBN 0-942784-27-8 • **$19.95**	______
______	***Work in the New Economy:*** *Careers and Job Seeking into the 21st Century*, Robert Wegmann • ISBN 0-942784-19-7 • **$14.95**	______
______	***The Occupational Outlook Handbook*** • ISBN 0-942784-38-3 • **$17.95**	______
______	***The Career Connection:*** *Guide to College Majors and Their Related Careers*, Dr. Fred Rowe • ISBN 0-942784-82-0 • **$15.95**	______
______	***The Career Connection II:*** *Guide to Technical Majors and Their Related Careers*, Dr. Fred Rowe • ISBN 0-942784-83-9 • **$13.95**	______
	Subtotal	______
	Sales Tax	______
	Shipping: *($3 for first book, $1 for each additional book.)*	______
	(U.S. Currency only) **TOTAL ENCLOSED WITH ORDER**	______

(Prices subject to change without notice)

❑ Check ❑ Money order ❑ Credit Card: ❑ MasterCard ❑ VISA ❑ AMEX

Card # (If Applies)______________________________ Exp. Date__________

Name (Please Print)______________________________

Name of Organization (if applies)______________________________

Address______________________________

City/State/Zip______________________________

Daytime Telephone (   )________-______________________

Thank you for your order!